Praise for Cultivate

Rural leaders are no strangers to the forces of nature. The past two years of pandemic though, have asked new things of all of us in virtually every aspect of our lives. How and where we work has been transformed. But this book is not about working in a COVID environment. It's about a redefinition of what makes a high functioning team that puts our humanity at the centre of productivity. This book challenges leaders to pay careful attention to cultivate their own well-being and those whom they lead. It provides the tools to cultivate the courage, compassion and psychological safety which allows leaders and their teams to truly thrive.

Dr Helen Haines MP, Independent Federal Member for Indi

In my early work-life as I navigated a career in rural Australia, I was well-schooled by my peers (predominantly male) in what is now clearly an archaic and arguably, authoritarian approach to leadership. As a newbie, I guess I bought into this method also as I saw it played out over and again in my dealings with other similar organisations and rural enterprises. It was all around me! The stakes were high, the risks were real and therefore a task-leadership approach was what appeared to work best. At the same time, I witnessed numerous industry colleagues endure relationship breakdowns, health issues, work-life imbalance and ultimately burn-out. It was confronting and confusing. Certainly, I did not envisage or had wished for this when I first embarked on my own professional journey in agriculture. With some honesty I questioned how I would ever 'make it,' when intrinsically I knew that it did not reflect who I was or wanted to be. There was no comfort in that.

Gladly over the years, there has been an evolution playing out for us all working in rural industry. There has been a growth in diversity of thought (and thankfully gender!) about what effective leadership can be, hence Cynthia's book is timely in building on this promise. So that new and emerging rural leaders have a reference which reinforces the human element and those characteristics which deliver uniqueness and harmony within us as individuals and as teams working together.

This book provides the framework, scientific backing and reflection opportunities for us to engage better with ourselves and to help us 'cultivate' working relationships which are meaningful and trusting. As a leader there is an important difference between communicating with others because we feel they have something of value to say, versus communicating because we believe they have value. Cynthia's book makes this distinction very clear and why it is so critically important.

Ged Sippel, Vegetable Seeds Business Unit Head (Japan, Australasia, Korea), Syngenta

This book is for rural, regional and remote leaders, and people for whom the old way of teams, leadership and organisations no longer works. This book is for young people in rural Australia who are doing it differently and no longer want to learn to fit into the old way of thinking.

Cultivate celebrates people as our greatest resource. It will support you to operate more creatively, courageously, and wisely in mobilising collaboration and innovation. It will support you to adapt to thrive in tomorrow's world.

Lynne Strong, CEO Action4Agriculture

Rural leaders face many challenges and obstacles, all having an impact on their own well-being, which has a domino effect on their leadership, decision-making and the well-being of those they lead.

This book will not only give you the tools and structure to thrive as a rural leader, but also to cultivate positive well-being in those around you, so they can thrive and become leaders also.

Warren Davies, speaker, mental health advocate, www.theunbreakablefarmer.com.au

Cultivate was such a pleasure to read. I couldn't put it down and ended up reading it over two evenings – it was easy to read and had a good flow. The frameworks Cynthia created helped me understand the concepts and pulled everything together. It was great having reflection space after each chapter. I loved the quotes at the start of each chapter. It made the book very inspiring and the design is bright and bubbly – just like the author!

Congratulations on creating a wonderful gift and tool for regional and rural leaders. There are so many nuggets of gold throughout the entire book. I'd recommend this book to anyone who is wanting to improve their leadership skills.

Den Lim, Community Programs Coordinator at GippSport, Traralgon VIC

Cynthia delivers a compelling science-based case around the need for a human-centric approach or Cultivated leadership. You will be encouraged to walk down the hall of mirrors and reflect on choices that either add or subtract happiness to your life and flow-on impacts to the people closest to you.

Cynthia's lived experiences in rural and regional Australia add context to the premise – Cultivated Leadership is most impactful. Cynthia highlights behaviours we should strive for and hope others around us display. Being a leader in rural Australia has many similarities to urban Australia. Still, Cultivated leadership is more critical when living and working in rural Australia.

Don't read what I say. Read this book. It will add far more value to your life.

Chris Sounness, Executive Director, Wimmera Development Association

What a great read, and beautifully constructed. I loved the evidence base throughout and enjoyed the anecdotes and examples. Cultivate is a most excellent title for the process Cynthia takes the reader through. It really drew me in. Each story and context resonated with my experience of living and leading rurally.

Tricia Currie, CEO Women's Health Loddon Mallee

Everyone is a leader to someone, somewhere at some time. This book will help you develop the skills needed to lead, but not just to lead, but to cultivate – firstly yourself and then the way that you interact with others. And don't forget a good cultivator replaces him or herself and in a positive way!

Di Bowles, dairy farmer and board member

With her trademark warmth and wisdom, Cynthia invites us on a journey of re-imagining what it is to be an effective workplace leader. This is a practical guide to achieving results whilst retaining the heart of rural values.

Dr Skye Charry (Associate Professor of Law, University of New England / Author 'Whispers from the Bush, The Workplace Sexual Harassment of Australian Rural Women')

Cultivate

Cultivate

How neuroscience and well-being support rural leaders to thrive

cynthia mahoney

Cultivate

How neuroscience and well-being support rural leaders to thrive

Published by Cynthia Mahoney
First published in 2021 in Melbourne, Australia

www.cynthiamahoney.com.au
Melbourne, Victoria

Edited by Jenny Magee
Cover illustration by Tjaša Žurga Žabkar
Typeset and printed in Australia by BookPOD

ISBN: 978-0-6453551-0-9 (paperback)
ISBN: 978-0-6453551-1-6 (ebook)

A catalogue record for this book is available from the National Library of Australia

Dedication

This book, my first, is dedicated to the ones I love. It's a long list!

I have always been aware that I hit the jackpot in life to be born to my wonderful parents, Anne and Gerard Mahoney. I never take that for granted. Their unconditional love, encouragement, support, generosity and belief in me throughout my life is the ultimate example of how to apply a cultivating approach to life. When you know you are truly loved, you can do anything. They taught me to be true to myself (even when it's hard), stand up for what is right and navigate life with colour, joy and fun.

To my brothers Jules and Josh and sister-in-law Vanessa, I don't know where I would be without you. I know I can always count on my darling younger brothers to keep me honest, call me out, try to keep me from taking myself too seriously. They challenge me, are fiercely loyal and always have my back – as I have theirs. Ness, I'm forever grateful you're my sister-in-law. You are such a special person – strong, kind, creative, thoughtful, generous and just fabulous to be around.

My nieces Georgia and Lila, and nephew Clem, inspire me every day. I'm so proud of the intelligent, caring, thoughtful, and totally fun humans they are. I want the world to be a better place for them. Where they are safe to express themselves fully and are valued for who they are and what they do. I believe a cultivating approach can deliver this for them.

You learn a lot about each other when the chips are down, and your backs are against the wall. I am eternally proud and grateful for how our little family banded together and rowed in the same direction in the years of Mum's illness and after her death. It's been hard without her, but we're all still here for each other, led by the example she set.

To my tribe of beloved friends – the goddesses, the PLC girls, the Benalla girls, the Geelong Cat-lovers, the ex-DPI crew, Women in Ag buddies, our gorgeous network of family friends, my awesome neighbours and other fabulous random peeps I've been fortunate enough to meet along the way – thank you all so much. I'm a lucky woman to have you in my life! In memory, too, of those friends no longer with us, including Pete, Nic, Jane and Tan. Forever in my heart.

I would never have written this book without inspiration and expectations from the Thought Leaders Business School community. Matt, Lisa, Pete, Col, Paul M, Kate, Ruth, Paige, Gayle, Maree and countless others. Thank you for setting the bar high, being so generous, and helping people like me achieve things they never thought possible. It's so important to seek out people who inspire you to lift your game – you can't be it if you can't see it!

Thank you to my generous friend Miffy Gilbert who read the first draft of the book and provided such helpful feedback and perspectives.

Thank you to my superstar (and patient) business manager Niki Flood, who manages to work with my ad hoc ways, for all your wonderful support. I'm so appreciative of all you do.

To Cath Connell from Wholehearted Marketing (the name says it all!) for all your terrific work on the book illustrations and graphics – love it!

To Sylvie Blair from BookPoD, who made my words look wonderful on the page.

To my editor Jenny Magee – thank you for holding my hand and finding a process for writing this book that worked for me. It took a while, but we got there in the end through your fabulous coaching and encouragement!

And finally, to my amazing clients, colleagues and mentors from many different walks of life, including those of you who generously allowed me to share your stories in this book. I learn so much from you and love working with you. It's such a privilege to do work I am passionate about and to know that we are on the same page. Together we are making the world better!

xxx Cynthia

PS To my fur family, Alfie (Alfred Gary Ablett Mahoney), the cavoodle, and Lulu (Princess Lulu), the cat, I've really had to lift my leadership game with you two and step up to be the leader you need me to be. Alfie, please remember I am the top dog. Louie, I will always be your willing slave.

Contents

INTRODUCTION

Challenges for Rural and Regional Leaders

'All great changes are preceded by chaos. The disruption we see in the world is the prelude to emergence. Let's all commit to a more peaceful, just, sustainable, healthier, and happier world. We must become what we wish to see by transcending our limited tribal identities.'

Deepak Chopra

(Chopra, 2018)

Mel understood the challenges faced by rural and regional leaders all too well. Her community had been in drought for several years, and, as the local agronomist, she was asked about the weather forecast wherever she went. Mel is like the local doctor who can never go anywhere without people talking about their ailments.

Growers confided their worries and stresses as the drought wrought havoc on farm finances and spread to other businesses in the town. People Mel had worked with for many years suffered strains on their mental health. In her role as agronomist and community leader, she felt under enormous pressure to stay calm, listen, offer some hope and keep giving good advice to help farmers manage through the drought.

What no one realised, though, was that Mel's own mental health was suffering badly. The pressure of constantly being the person that the community looked to for strength and support had taken its toll. She was at breaking point. Mel needed help, so she made an appointment with her local doctor.

Stepping into the waiting room, Mel tried to keep it all together until she saw the doctor. But she was greeted by a couple of local farmers and a nurse (who was married to a farmer). 'Hey Mel,' said one accusingly, 'You told us last week it was going to rain, and it hasn't!' 'Yeah, Mel', said the nurse, 'How could you do that?'

Mel was devastated. In the middle of a personal mental health emergency, she was abused in what should have been a safe space. The community that was usually so supportive was adding to her stress. She felt she was failing and judged. For her own well-being, Mel started to withdraw from the community to look after herself.

Sound familiar? You may know someone like Mel but not recognise the stress and strains they are under.

Rural leadership is public

Leadership is always full of challenges, but after more than twenty-five years of working with rural, regional and remote leaders (from here on, I will refer to this collective as rural leaders), I've found that these leaders contend with additional and different challenges from their city counterparts.

Rural leaders often live in the same community where they work, so there is nowhere to hide. They always have to be on, and it's hard to switch off because, wherever they go, people always talk about work. If they make a professional decision that negatively affects someone, they will likely see that person at footy, church or school. They will probably also have to face their extended family and friends. One rural leader felt he couldn't terminate a toxic team member because they played in the same cricket team, and life would have just been too difficult.

Because they're so well known, they are under pressure to be authentic. You can't have separate work and community personas because everyone knows you. Senior leaders I worked with in the city could be ruthless and hard-nosed at work, then go home and be entirely different people – caring and considerate.

As a rural leader, you often see the results of hard decisions firsthand and must be present to be accountable. You can't leave work and go home a few suburbs away to another identity where you don't see people you work with. An urban leader usually only needs to lead in an immediate work context, whereas rural leaders, particularly in small communities, wear many hats and carry a weightier leadership load. Unlike in urban areas, rural leaders are also considered role models (Doshi, 2017).

Rural leaders are greatly connected to and influenced by the physical environment in which they live – particularly the exposure to natural disasters. Consider some of the recent challenges – bushfires, drought, floods, COVID-19 and mice plagues.

In 2019, I attended the Australian Women in Agriculture Conference in Ballina, New South Wales, where there was lush grass, a beautiful river and the majestic sea. I met women who had not seen green grass for years. The effect of that on your psyche and mental health is enormous. Many women took off their shoes and stood barefoot in the grass, revelling in its feeling on their skin. They were mentally uplifted and filled with joy at the relief of seeing things growing instead of the desolate, dust-filled, barren lands that surrounded them back home.

The personal cost is high

Rural leaders often manage staff who, like themselves, are involved in volunteer organisations like the Country Fire Authority or State Emergency Service. Their businesses and community commitment are entwined. If the environment is suffering, your staff and your community suffer too. When a few events pile on top of each other, widespread and cumulative stress and trauma can occur. That's a lot for a leader to bear.

If rural leaders have a different opinion from the general flow of the community, the consequences can affect them and their families, and they can face exclusion and social isolation.

One farming woman I know decided to get involved in a national policy committee to try to make a positive difference for her community. She had identified a proposed change and decided to get involved and influence rather than just protest against it. She spoke out and tried to get the community on board, but the backlash saw friends turn their backs, and threats and abuse directed towards her family. The small community she had been part of since birth turned on her. In the end, the cost was too great, so she resigned from the committee.

Rural leaders need to navigate and respond to the mental health issues of people in their organisations, industries and communities. While people experience mental health issues at a similar rate (twenty per cent) across Australia, the rates of self-harm and suicide increase with remoteness. The rate of suicide in rural and regional areas is forty per cent higher than in major cities. It increases to fifty per cent in remote areas.

While rural people are conditioned for rural stoicism, toughing it out can make it harder to ask for help. There can be a fear of stigma around mental health, and people living in smaller communities may feel more visible and worry about confidentiality (National Rural Health Alliance Inc, 2017).

The pressure on rural women

Women in rural and regional areas are far more likely to experience disadvantage and discrimination in the workplace (and in society more broadly) than women in urban areas near big cities. A 2017 report released by the Australian Human Rights Commission found that intersectional women (for example, women from CALD backgrounds, women who identify as LGBTQI+, Aboriginal and Torres Strait Islander women and women with a disability) were more likely to face further discrimination in rural and regional towns. Consequently, it can be more challenging for women to break into leadership in rural and regional areas. Isolation and close community ties also mean it is harder to speak up if women experience discrimination, harassment or violence (Australian Human Rights Commission, 2017).

One of my coaching clients explained her experience of leadership like this.

'Throughout my entire career in horticulture and agriculture, I've been patronised and my contribution minimised. When working in the retail sector in the city, this wasn't the case. There were far more women and diversity in leadership roles, and our contribution was valued and recognised. I'm only "allowed" to sit on some industry boards and committees because there isn't a man who wants the spot.

'I'd like to stand as chair of a board I'm on – but I know the nomination won't be supported. It's doubly frustrating when I know I'm one of the most capable people in the room, and yet they look right through me. I'm the only female on the board.

'Lack of role models means my leadership vision for myself is small. Any role models that have been there, I've seen how they get treated. This doesn't encourage me to strive for the same treatment. There is no obvious circuit-breaker in the current climate.'

The path to well-being in leadership

To achieve sustainable leadership in rural areas, we need a cultivating style of leadership that puts well-being at the centre of work. The extra pressures on rural and regional leaders make nurturing, nourishing and leading with a human-centred approach an even higher priority.

The extra pressures on rural and regional leaders make nurturing, nourishing and leading with a human-centred approach an even higher priority.

Matt Linnegar, chief executive of the Australian Rural Leadership Foundation, put it like this. 'There are always people who think that a different leadership style could be more successful – more aggressive, more combative, more coercive. Can you get results with that approach? Absolutely you can get results. My question over a long time of being involved is, how sustainable is it? You can do that and get some short-term advantage but is that to the long-term greater good that you're serving?' (Philanthropy Australia, 2021).

This book is for you

This book is for rural, regional and remote leaders, and people for whom the old way of teams, leadership and organisations no longer works. It is for those who want a more human-centred way of working. A place where employees are free to be themselves without judgement or punishment, use their strengths and flourish at work and in life.

If you want to be authentic, lead with the heart and with emotional courage, be OK with asking for help and offering help, talk about struggles and be supported in the times when life isn't easy, this book is for you.

It is written with love, appreciation and validation, honouring your experience and what you have still to contribute.

Cultivate is a call to action for all who share a well-being, human-centred approach. Creating positive change that benefits ourselves, our people, our industries and our communities starts with you, one step at a time.

It is also for leaders who are frustrated that, despite their best efforts, they haven't been able to tap into their people's potential and achieve the outcomes they need. This may show up when they ask questions in meetings, and no one speaks, or a lack of staff initiative or innovation despite encouragement. It may appear in the conflict that has people talking behind each other's backs rather than addressing it openly. We see a lack of accountability, poor morale and patchy performance. Errors occur, while inefficiencies negatively affect growth and profit.

Leadership can be a really tough gig.

The ideas in this book are just that, based on research that I, and others, have found helpful. They include real-life examples of cultivating human-centred and well-being leadership styles from people I've worked with. They have inspired me as a facilitator and coach. This is backed up by the latest findings from neuroscience that show how leaders can create brain-friendly environments to get the best out of people. I want to resource rural and regional leaders to be neuro-leaders and add this skill set to their toolkit.

This book also includes real-life examples of what not to do. They are behaviours and actions that we want to eliminate from work, industries and communities. In talking with people about these, I heard clearly that some of the dominant behaviours currently displayed by some leaders are not up to scratch.

None of this suggests that you are personally not good enough or that you are failing if you don't try them. This book is not another reason to whip yourself! My ultimate message is about the need to cultivate well-being and put humans at the centre of work. It is about compassion and generosity. It's OK not to be OK. You're human, and you won't always get it right. You have permission to get it wrong! You are enough.

PART ONE

We Need a New Story of Leadership

'The challenge of leadership is to be strong, but not rude; be kind, but not weak; be bold, but not bully; be thoughtful, but not lazy; be humble, but not timid; be proud, but not arrogant; have humor, but without folly.'

Jim Rohn

(Wolfson, 2017

1

'You have brains in your head
You have feet in your shoes
You can steer yourself
Any direction you choose.
You'll be on your way up!
You'll be seeing great sights!
You'll join the high fliers
Who soar to great heights.'

Dr Seuss

(Seuss, 1990)

One of my favourite stories of all time is ***Oh the Places You'll Go*** by Dr Seuss (Seuss, 1990).

It tells the story of how a person starts their life ready to go to great places. They stride confidently into the future, ready to start exploring the world with endless possibilities awaiting them.

You have brains in your head
You have feet in your shoes
You can steer yourself
Any direction you choose.
You'll be on your way up!
You'll be seeing great sights!
You'll join the high fliers
Who soar to great heights.

Sounds like a high performer, doesn't it? Someone you'd want in your team. Being their best self. Living their best life. Being productive. Kicking goals. Delivering outcomes. It seems their performance will follow this trajectory:

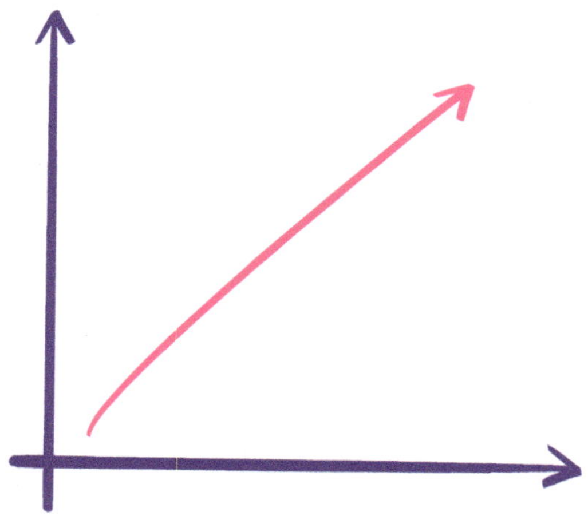

Figure 1: Perceived high performer life trajectory

Until it doesn't. Until life happens.

Everyone's life journey graph is different. Ups and downs. Swings and roundabouts. Peaks and troughs. Two steps forward, ten steps back. Onwards and upwards. Stuck. Paused. Growing. Shining. Stagnating. Falling. Failing. Winning. Losing. In flow. High-performing. Resting. Recovering. Unwell. Healthy. Happy. Sad. Surviving. Thriving. Rejected. Loved. Disappointed. Chaotic.

Perhaps it might look more like this:

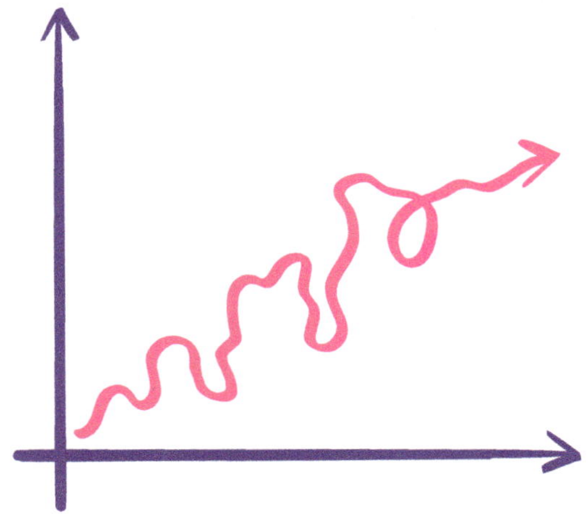

Figure 2: Real human life trajectory

What would your life journey and trajectory look like if you were to map it? What about for others on your team or in your organisation? Do you even know?

This book started as a guide for leaders to build, nurture and nourish high-performing teams. It has long been my passion to create workplaces where people show up as their best selves and make a great contribution.

As I've dug deeper and done more reflecting, I've realised the very notion of looking at work through the lens of high performance sounds exhausting and could be demotivating and overwhelming and unrealistic. I've always been interested in well-being, as I know from personal experience that you need to look after yourself or you won't be able to help anyone else. Yet, I was unsure if organisations would value well-being.

Isn't it time we busted the myth that we must create high-performing individuals, teams and leaders? Is using this language contributing to mental health issues, psychological safety concerns and unrealistic organisational expectations that lead to burnout, disengagement and presenteeism?

> It has long been my passion to create workplaces where people show up as their best selves and make a great contribution.

Is it time to evolve beyond high performance and embrace a style that places well-being first? One that is more fit-for-purpose and reflects the complexities, challenges and pressures of the modern world we live and work in?

I think the answer is a resounding, 'Hell, yes'.

Reflection questions

What resonated with you in this chapter?

What insights do you have?

What could you cultivate (grow more of)?

What could you eliminate (do less of)?

If you did this, how would your life be different?

If you did this, who else would benefit?

How would they benefit?

If you don't make a change, what are the consequences?

2

From High Performance to Whole Human

'Hard work is important. So are play and non-productivity. My worth is tied not to my productivity but to my existence. I am worthy of rest.'

Glennon Doyle

(Doyle, 2020)

High performance stress

What comes up for you when you think about high performance? What about a high-performing individual? A high-performing team? A high-performing leader? A high-performing culture?

Until recently, I assumed that we should all aspire to high performance – in ourselves, our teams, leadership, and culture. However, the pandemic has disrupted many traditional work norms, and it's now obvious that what used to work as high-performance culture is not fit-for-purpose in the world in which we now find ourselves. It's time to evolve to a well-being-focused and human-centred world that is much more sustainable for us all.

The thesaurus likens high performance to terms like 'high-octane', 'gassed up', 'high speed', 'pumped up' and 'supercharged'. It's described as 'having the quality of performing exceptionally well. Accomplishing, implementing, executing, actioning, activity, fulfilling, perfecting, completing, accomplishing, attaining' (Thesaurus, 2013).

A high-performance work team refers to a 'group of goal-focused individuals with specialised expertise and complementary skills who collaborate, innovate and produce consistently superior results. The group relentlessly pursues performance excellence through shared goals, shared leadership, collaboration, open communication, clear role expectations and group operating rules, early conflict resolution, and a strong sense of accountability and trust among its members' (Penhart, 2020).

Does that seem like a sustainable or realistic state of being to you? Particularly the 'relentlessly pursuing performance excellence' part.

Leadership expert Daniel Goleman described six leadership styles in his classic HBR article, ***Leadership That Gets Results***

(Goleman, 2000). Pacesetting is one. It's where a leader sets high standards for performance and is driven to achieve. High performance can have an air of pacesetting about it, but Goleman says this style should be used sparingly. His research found that while pacesetting sounds admirable and you would think that this approach would improve results, it actually destroys organisational climate and can negatively affect employee morale. That is because a leader who predominantly uses this style sets and works to extremely high standards that they also expect from their team. It can be relentless, overwhelming and stressful. And guess what? Neuroscience tells us that humans don't perform at their best when they are stressed! But more on the science behind stress later.

As Carl Lindberg described, there are definite disadvantages to a pacesetting leader or culture (Lindburg, 2021):

- Employees are stressed and overwhelmed
- Trust is lost
- Work can be repetitive and boring
- Employees receive little or no feedback
- Employee engagement is low
- Pacesetting can become part of a system.

A high-performance culture also sounds very one-dimensional. That is, we only have one way of doing things, and that's the high-performing way. It doesn't accommodate life's challenges.

And what about when you're not high-performing? How do we describe the opposite? Failing. Faulty. Shoddy. Unsatisfactory. Inadequate. Dismal. Unfit. Ineffective. Neglect (Thesaurus, 2013).

Wow. That sounds harsh, doesn't it? I don't know about you, but I can't operate at high speed or be supercharged or take action all the time. So, where does that leave me if I'm not continually high-performing at the standard I should aim for? Probably feeling anxious, under pressure, afraid, shamed, unsafe, an imposter?

That is not a healthy way to live. More than forty-one per cent of millennials and forty-six per cent of Gen Zs report feeling stressed all or most of the time (Deloitte, 2021).

Even elite athletes need regular periods of rest and recovery. They aim for moments of high performance rather than a continual state of being.

This brings me to the second problem I'm having with the term 'high performance'. The alternative definition involves putting on a show. Play acting. Posing. Posturing. Pretending. Showing off. Dramatising. Feigning. Mimicking (Thesaurus, 2013).

There is an element of pretence in this. Of being inauthentic. That there's pressure to act like we're high-performing even if we're not. The subliminal message here is that it's not OK not to be OK.

It gets personal

At a particularly difficult time, I was running my own leadership practice, and my mother had just died from ovarian cancer after four and a half years of illness. I was also going through peri-menopause, had developed anxiety and was fatigued, emotionally spent and run down.

I told my psychologist, 'I'm a leadership facilitator. I'm all about high performance, leading yourself and being your best self, despite the challenges you face. But right now, I'm really struggling, and I can't get myself out of it. I should be able to, though. I feel like such a fraud and a failure.'

My psychologist looked at me with such compassion and said, gently and firmly, 'Cynthia, that is all totally fine when everything is relatively normal. But things for you just aren't normal right now. It's OK to be feeling as you are.'

It was such a relief. To have her accept me as I was and not judge me as failing. I was so fortunate to be running my own business and in charge of my destiny, but I needed deep rest and recovery. I needed to reduce my workload. I needed time to grieve. And I was able to give myself this.

Luckily my work filled my cup and was nurturing, fulfilling and uplifting. It didn't take much from me. I was open with my clients about what was going on and had their acceptance, support and understanding. I was also studying leadership and coaching, which was very nurturing and provided a supportive network. But I needed to go gently, compassionately and carefully with work, study and life while navigating the personal storm.

I remember thinking that I was lucky to be my own boss and not in an organisation. I just couldn't imagine that what I was going through would be accepted or tolerated at my previous workplace. There would have been a sense of, 'Enough. Just get on with it'. I would have felt ashamed and that I was letting the team down. I would have needed to hide how I was feeling to survive. That being my authentic self and admitting my struggle was not OK. I am not sure that the organisation's leaders would have looked at me with compassion either – I feel it would have been more like exasperation and judgement.

The price of performance

The consequences of pursuing an unrealistic expectation of high performance as a continual state of being in the workplace are playing out right now in the form of unwell, disengaged employees and rising mental health problems.

Global analytics firm Gallup has found that around seventy

per cent of employees are struggling or suffering rather than thriving in their overall lives. Eighty per cent of employees are not engaged or actively disengaged at work. This doesn't just have a human cost to these employees and their families; it also has an economic cost. Lack of engagement costs the global economy US$8.1 trillion, nearly ten per cent of GDP, in lost productivity each year.

In their *State of the Global Workplace 2021*, Gallup chair Jim Clifton, asked, 'What if the next global crisis is a mental health pandemic? It is here now. Negative emotions – worry, stress, anger and sadness – among employees worldwide reached record levels in 2020. These problems existed long before COVID-19. Gallup has discovered that negative emotions have been rising over the past decade. Even if we return to pre-COVID-19 levels of these emotions, the trends are still concerning' (Gallup, 2021).

Eighty per cent of employees are not engaged or actively disengaged at work.

Reflection questions

What resonated with you in this chapter?

What insights do you have?

What could you cultivate (grow more of)?

What could you eliminate (do less of)?

If you did this, how would your life be different?

If you did this, who else would benefit?

How would they benefit?

If you don't make a change, what are the consequences?

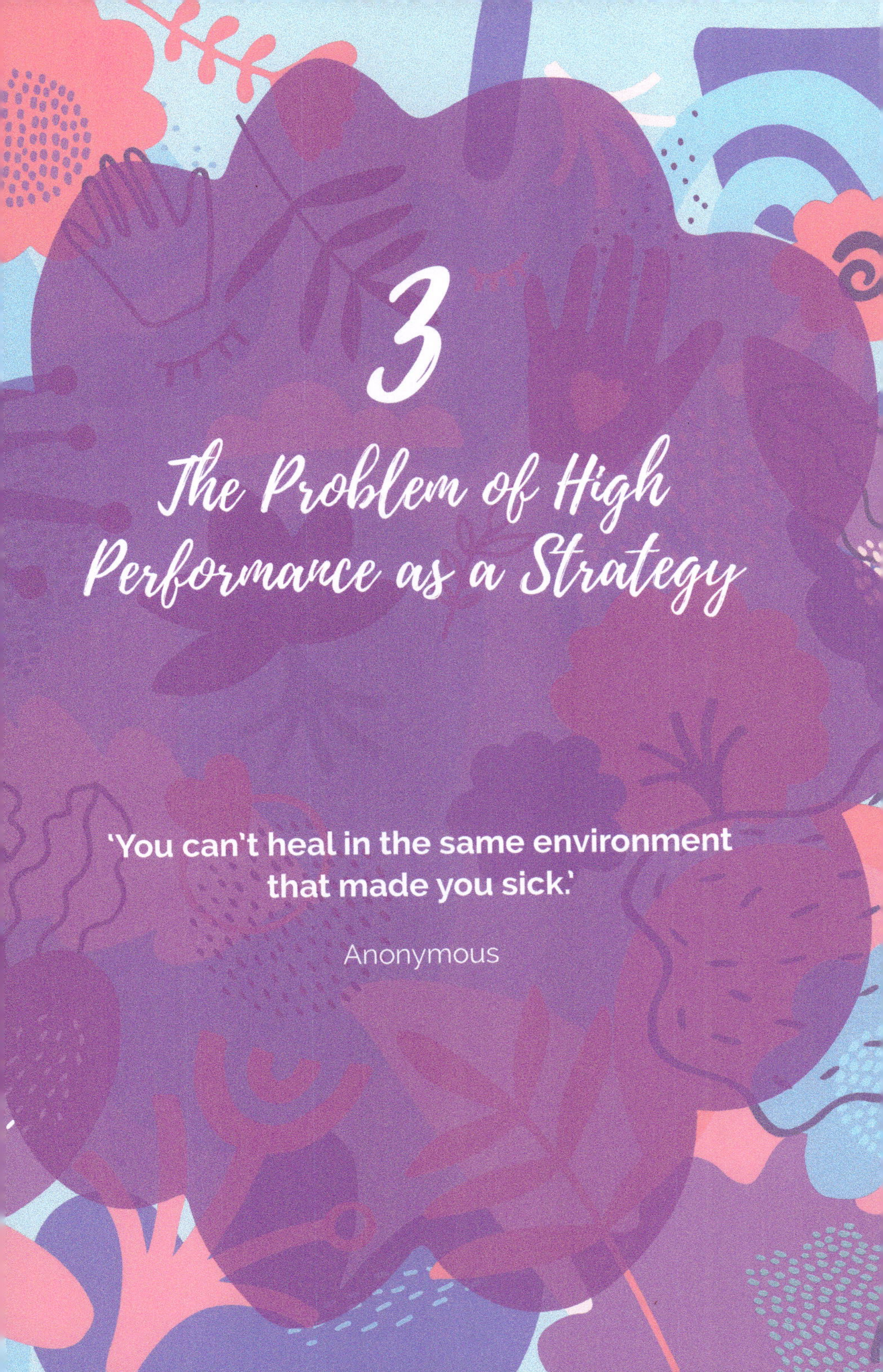

3

The Problem of High Performance as a Strategy

'You can't heal in the same environment that made you sick.'

Anonymous

Time to rethink

High performance is an outcome – not a strategy or process for leading a team or an organisation. The irony is that using high performance as a game plan means it becomes its own worst enemy, leading to disengagement, stress, resentment and burnout. All of which end up costing organisations through lost productivity, increased staff turnover, inefficient teams, increased risk, reduced growth and profits, projects not keeping to time and budget, poor staff morale, poor customer service, lack of innovation, and more.

Making high performance your leadership, team or culture strategy won't get you where you want to go.

Making high performance your leadership, team or culture strategy won't get you where you want to go.

The pandemic has busted some myths about how we work, particularly that people can't be trusted to work productively from home. Overnight, all our excuses for why we couldn't do certain things disappeared as businesses and governments just made it happen.

It's now time to dismantle the continual pursuit of high performance as an organisational strategy. The pandemic has brought into sharp focus the importance of employee well-being and the need to make this front and centre of work.

Dr Michelle McQuaid has conducted extensive research into well-being at work and believes it is in employers' interests to look for ways to support employees. When well-being is high, we are more productive and bring more energy, focus and motivation to our work which is mutually beneficial for employers and employees (The Well-Being Lab, 2021). High performance is an outcome of pursuing a well-being and human-first strategy. Ah, the irony!

Gallup found that career well-being has the most significant impact on people's overall state. We can't thrive without a good job and career. Career well-being is the foundation of our best possible life. Their extensive research has also found that 'my job' and 'my manager' have the greatest impact on thriving. Gallup's *State of the Globe 2021* report found that across Australia and New Zealand:

- Forty-five per cent of us experience stress daily (an increase of five per cent since 2019)
- Fifty-seven per cent of us are thriving (a decrease of seven per cent since 2019)
- And only twenty per cent are engaged at work (an increase of one per cent since 2019) (Gallup, 2021).

Working from home in COVID connected our work and home lives, reminding us of what matters most, which, for many, is family, health, well-being, time to exercise, flexibility and connection.

Ironically, it has always been that way, but we seem to have lost touch with that part by keeping work and home separate. COVID also reminded us that we bring our range of human emotions when we show up for work. Much that happens in life affects our work, and COVID made it OK to share that and be more real. Again – it has always been like that, but we didn't show it.

The evidence is real

I've been facilitating many online check-ins to keep people connected during their physical isolation. People need to have space to stop, reflect and talk honestly about how things are going for them – to talk about the conditions in which they are running their marathon. Some things I've been hearing people say are:

- Working at home with two toddlers is really hard
- I'm struggling without routine
- I'm finding it hard to draw a line between work and home
- I can't see my grandchildren; I miss everyone, I miss the little things
- I'm doing OK, but my partner has been made redundant, and I don't know how to help her
- My teenage son is struggling with his mental health in lockdown, and it's hard to know what to do
- It's the unknown that gets to me – I feel really overwhelmed
- It's been a real roller coaster; it's OK, and then it's not OK
- I have good days and bad days. I'm a hugger, so I'm missing physical contact
- My child has special needs, and she is finding the lack of routine hard. I'm working early in the morning and late at night, so I can be with her during the day
- For me working from home is easy. Working from home with kids and not having the odd relief that grandparents offer? That's hard
- I'm actually doing OK, just a bit over Zoom meetings, but proud of how our team is handling things.

It's as though a curtain has lifted and two worlds have collided.

People want to integrate them. I'm reminded of the Wizard of Oz, where the great and powerful Oz turned out to be just a little old bloke behind a curtain. In other words, we pretend that we are high-performing, but it turns out we are simply humans hiding our struggles.

The path of high performance and the continual need for more has led us to this point where people are sick. We need well people at work who can be human, curious, courageous, and collaborative to solve the world's problems and realise the opportunities.

The model of high performance looks pretty mechanical, clinical and engineered, and people aren't machines. It doesn't leave much room for individuals to be human with bad days, bad months and bad years. There's nothing about the heart, compassion or kindness. Humans are messy. Life is messy.

Can we do this in the workplace, though? Is there another way of being? High performance has got us to this point, but can we evolve and use a process of cultivating where well-being and the whole human are at the centre of our personal development, teams, leadership approach, and organisational and industry cultures? This will set us up for personal and business success in our rapidly-changing world. It will get us to where we need to be.

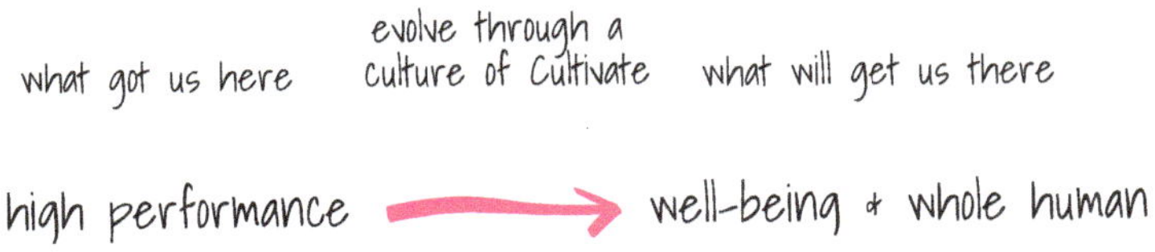

what got us here
evolve through a culture of Cultivate
what will get us there
high performance
well-being + whole human

Figure 3: Evolving to a cultivating culture

Reflection questions

What resonated with you in this chapter?

What insights do you have?

What could you cultivate (grow more of)?

What could you eliminate (do less of)?

If you did this, how would your life be different?

If you did this, who else would benefit?

How would they benefit?

If you don't make a change, what are the consequences?

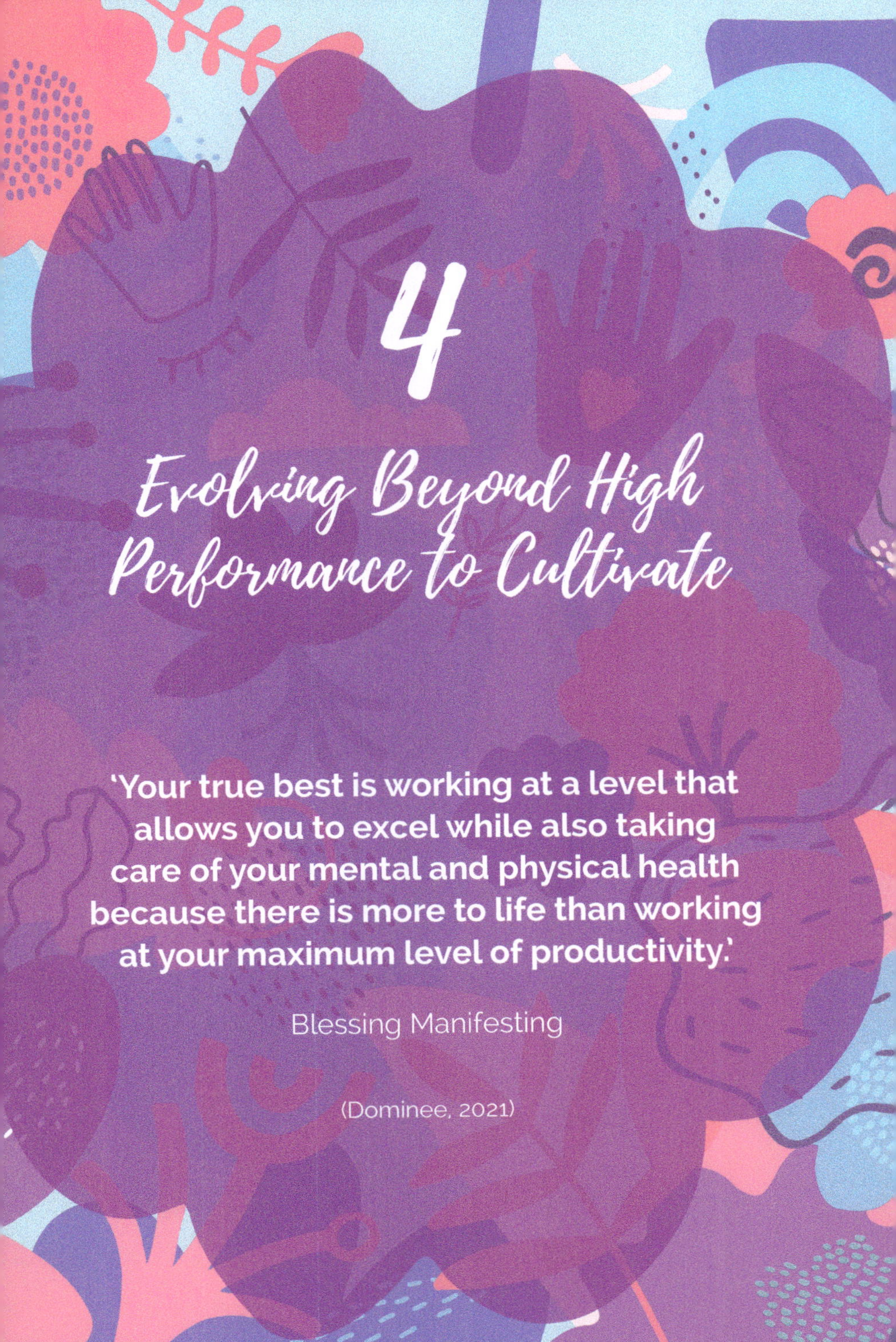

4

Evolving Beyond High Performance to Cultivate

'Your true best is working at a level that allows you to excel while also taking care of your mental and physical health because there is more to life than working at your maximum level of productivity.'

Blessing Manifesting

(Dominee, 2021)

Cultivate is a choice

If we think of high performance as an outcome of leading teams and developing cultures rather than an operating model in the workplace, what might support high performance while avoiding burnout, disengagement, and illness?

I'd like to propose a new model, or rather a process, of cultivating. The word 'cultivate' means nourishing, nurturing, cherishing, fostering, promoting, improving, fertilising, advancing, encouraging, improving by labour, care or study, and refining.

High performance can be a self-defeating prophecy for many well-intentioned leaders. We need a model of operating that is fit-for-purpose for the uncertain and changing times we live in. Business educator and coach Marshall Goldsmith wrote, 'What got you here won't get you there' (Goldsmith, 2008). The workplace cultures and behaviours that got us to this point will not take us where we need to go.

We also need a new way of operating that aligns with the values of the generations coming into the workforce. Gen Z and Millennials are more likely to shun companies and employers whose actions conflict with their personal values. They want a better planet, a fairer system and kinder humanity – and they are prepared to demand change.

More than a third of Millennials and Gen Zs expect the pandemic experiences to lead to a world that is more compassionate, more cooperative internationally, more altruistic, more able to tackle climate change. And they expect business to be more socially responsible (Deloitte, 2021).

Cultivate is the context in which caring leaders and teammates can enable people to be well at work and overcome the epidemic of stress and mental health issues. Burnout comes from high performance for its own sake and pursuing it as a continual state of being. Cultivate allows for the outcome of high performance but also the outcomes of rest, well-being, learning and failure. It is complex, multi-dimensional, courageous, authentic, human, and involves the heart. Cultivate reflects the diversity of the human experience, accepting that struggle is part of our experience and embracing it rather than pushing it down, gritting through or pretending it's not happening.

Cultivate has the long game in mind – it's about a sustainable way of being, while high performance is more a sprint than a marathon. With well-being at its centre, cultivation ensures that your people's batteries are continually recharging, with personal strategies, leaders that help them and a culture that affirms the importance of doing so.

It is a call to action for those who want a different way. We can create our own way, and it starts with you. Everyone is a leader. If you tackle problems with the same thinking with which you created them, you are doomed. Cultivate is validation for everyone for whom a combative, high-performance culture doesn't work. It is a shout out that it doesn't have to be that way.

We can create our own way, and it starts with you.

The cultivate model (figure 4) shows what it means to bring a cultivating process to our workplaces. We develop individuals with the knowledge, skills, tools and motivation to look after and cultivate themselves. We advance leaders who know how to look after themselves and constantly look for ways to cultivate their people. We establish cultivating cultures that encourage and support well-being and human beings, and where burnout is as harmful and old-school as smoking or not wearing seatbelts.

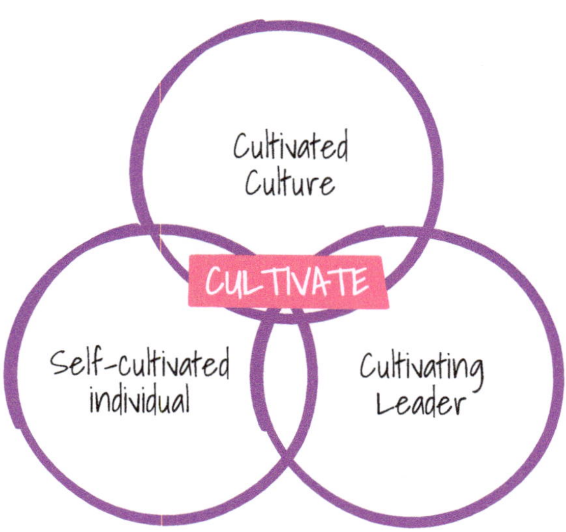

Figure 4: The cultivate model

Think about how you can achieve impact at three levels of change – culture, individuals and leaders. The sum of these parts cultivates and sustains well-being and human-centred workplaces, industries and communities.

Individuals shape leaders, who then forge culture. The same happens in reverse, where the culture influences the leaders who command the individuals. The culture shapes the individuals. The individual shapes the culture. Each part is connected and influences the others. To be a cultivated leader, you need first to understand how to be a self-cultivated person to support your people to do the same. Everyone must understand their role in shaping the culture through every action they take and how they choose to show up.

Figure 5: The relationship between culture, leaders and individuals

Research by McKinsey demonstrates that organisational change is inseparable from individual change. Change efforts often falter because individuals overlook the need to make fundamental changes in themselves. They found that 'half of all efforts to transform organisational performance fail either because senior managers don't act as role models for change or because people in the organisation defend the status quo. In other words, despite the stated change goals, people on the ground tend to behave as they did before' (Boaz & Fox, 2014).

So, three questions to ask yourself:

Do you have strategies in place to develop self-cultivating people? They will improve your ability to unlock and access everyone's best, so they are happier and higher performing.

Do you have strategies to develop cultivating leaders? They will improve leaders' ability to provide direction and support, engage effectively with the team and other stakeholders, and be accountable and deliver results.

Do you have strategies to develop a cultivated culture that also links individuals and leadership to the culture? They will ensure that leaders set your culture and all staff understand their role in supporting a culture where people feel safe, have permission to be themselves and where well-being is prioritised and operationalised effectively instead of being something we say but don't actually do.

Well-being is dynamic and constantly changing

I've developed a well-being ladder (figure 6) to represent the different states we operate in as we show up to work. It's simply not possible to be on our A-game all the time. Even elite athletes train to bring their best to moments of greatness rather than being in a constant state of excellence and high performance. As sporting careers are generally short in the context of their whole working life, athletes don't expect to operate at this level forever.

> By building cultivating cultures, we allow people to be like elastic bands – stretching and relaxing as they move up and down the ladder, without breaking.

It's important to remember that you constantly move around on the well-being ladder – it's dynamic. You can go up, down or jump levels within a moment, an hour, a day, and a life. You might be feeling overwhelmed, then talk with a friend and become clear and focused. You might be thriving and then suddenly overwhelmed when someone you love is diagnosed with a serious disease.

We need work environments that recognise this and allow flexible movement instead of expecting us to thrive. Reduce the pressure that sends people to burnout – it is much harder to move up the ladder from this position.

Figure 6: The well-being ladder

By building cultivating cultures, we allow people to be like elastic bands – stretching and relaxing as they move up and down the ladder, without breaking. And with practice and the right knowledge, tools, support, leadership and working environment, they will more often be relaxed and occasionally stretched – in a good way. In contrast, high performance conjures up the image of a band that is always stretched to breaking point.

How can we allow for the reality of people at different levels of the ladder in human-centred workplaces? How do we create environments where people can be well? That is, where it really is OK not to be OK, and you know you won't be judged, shamed or punished for being open about it. Where the ebbs and flows that are part of the human condition are accepted and embraced as part of the reality of playing the long game of sustainable performance.

Gallup defines thriving as 'good overall well-being'. They found that people who thrive have significantly fewer health problems and experience less worry, sadness, depression and anger. They are more hopeful, happier and energetic (Gallup, 2021).

At the other end of the ladder, the World Health Organization declared burnout an occupational phenomenon that undermines how well people perform at work. It is not experienced in other areas of life. WHO defined burnout as a 'syndrome conceptualized as resulting from chronic workplace stress that has not been successfully managed'. There are three key dimensions to burnout:

- Exhaustion: You feel depleted of energy, worn out, fatigued, or have overwhelming feelings of exhaustion
- Engagement: You feel emotionally distant and detached from your job or are negative or cynical about it
- Efficacy: You feel you're ineffective, your productivity and efficiency are reduced, you lack a sense of accomplishment, your morale is low, and you are unable to cope (World Health Organization, 2019).

Keeping things real

I facilitated a webinar on Creating a Mentally Healthy Workplace for a rural leadership team based right across Victoria. After sharing the well-being ladder, I asked them to discuss where they were personally located on the ladder and where they thought their teams were. Of the seven leaders present, five reported they were below the line in stress or overwhelm, and the other two shared that they were just above the line at surviving. None were anywhere near thriving.

And their teams? Collectively the leaders thought the teams they managed were hovering just above or just below the line. They identified some individuals who were doing OK and were resilient, clear and focused.

They considered their organisation's culture, where senior management still expected them to deliver unrealistic pre-COVID targets that involved numbers of farmers attending events. The organisation said all the right things by espousing that it was concerned about staff well-being. There were mental health seminars and encouragement to speak with the internal counsellor, yet staff were experiencing the exact opposite.

The team leaders saw that the caring sentiment was not conveyed in what the organisation expected from them. One received emails on a Sunday night from senior management asking for material to be delivered ASAP. Another was trying to protect his staff by encouraging them to look after themselves, yet the team knew that he was under enormous pressure and was not practising self-care.

They were still delivering on outcomes, so, to an outsider, it would have looked like a high-performing team with high-performing individuals. But behind the curtain, they definitely weren't Great and Powerful Wizards of Oz. They were struggling, and it wasn't sustainable. They were paying a massive price as a team and as individuals to keep up the pace.

Participating in the workshop was a cultivating process for the team. It allowed everyone to be OK as they were and to seek help. It gave them permission to be individuals who were struggling rather than high-performing. They were accepted rather than judged. It allowed them to be real.

If you know the story of the Velveteen Rabbit, this will resonate.

'Real isn't how you are made. It's a thing that happens to you. It doesn't happen all at once,' said the Skin Horse. 'You become. It takes a long time. That's why it doesn't happen often to people who break easily or have sharp edges, or who have to be carefully kept. Generally, by the time you are Real, most of your hair has been loved off, and your eyes drop out, and you get loose in the joints and very shabby. But these things don't matter at all, because once you are Real you can't be ugly, except to people who don't understand. Once you are Real you can't become unreal again. It lasts for always' (Bianco & Nicholson, 1975).

And what of the organisation? There is a massive cost when so many staff are not at their best. For example, one leader was planning to take time off as he was not coping, but that meant someone else in the team had to take on his role.

It is shocking to remember that burnout is caused by work.

Reflection questions

What resonated with you in this chapter?

What insights do you have?

What could you cultivate (grow more of)?

What could you eliminate (do less of)?

If you did this, how would your life be different?

If you did this, who else would benefit?

How would they benefit?

If you don't make a change, what are the consequences?

5

Neuro-leadership is the New Power Skill

'In these troubled, uncertain times, we don't need more command and control; we need better means to engage everyone's intelligence in solving challenges and crises as they arrive.'

Margaret J. Wheatley

(Wheatley M. J., 2005)

The evidence supports us

Years ago, I worked for a government department in a role that brought farming families together to talk about the future. It was one of the best jobs I've ever had, with families coming together to talk about their hopes and dreams, and understand how they communicated. It enabled them to have important conversations, navigate conflict and talk about finances, the environment and the people in their farming business.

There I honed my skills in group facilitation and learnt many valuable techniques that enabled a group to have conversations about things that mattered to them in a safe environment. This was years before any talk of neuroscience or understanding the role of psychological safety in how people perform. There wasn't language for such things. In our mainly science-based research, policy and extension organisation, some people saw our facilitation skills as fluffy, soft, airy-fairy and lacking in credibility. There was an attitude that 'Anyone can run a change or education program for farmers', or 'Anyone can facilitate a meeting or workshop'.

It has been exciting to see the emergence of neuroscience (the study of how our brains react in certain conditions) and its impact on how leaders and organisations approach change and working with people. Neuroscience has put scientific rigour behind many of the effective techniques that we used. They have proven powerful because they create brain-friendly environments where people can be at their best. And those icebreakers that many people found so cringeworthy? They build trust, create a safe environment and set up a group of people working together for success.

I'm on a mission to upskill rural leaders in the basics of neuroscience so we can get the best out of people and create environments where people can flourish. And guess what? The scientific research says that happier people are higher performing!

Happiness at work is win-win

Psychologist Shawn Achor is one of many researchers who have looked at the win-win outcomes from people being happier in the workplace. He found that 'the single greatest advantage in the modern economy is a happy and engaged workforce. A decade of research proves that happiness raises nearly every business and educational outcome: raising sales by thirty-seven per cent, productivity by thirty-one per cent, and accuracy on tasks by nineteen per cent, as well as a myriad of health and quality of life improvements. There's a big incentive for organisations to pay attention, as 'happiness leads to greater levels of profits' for companies that take the right steps (Achor, 2011).

Why would we not want to cultivate more happiness in the workplace if these are the results? What have we got to lose? Only burnout, stress, turnover, absenteeism, presenteeism, lower productivity, poor mental and physical health, and so the list goes on. It's a no-brainer.

As a leader, having a basic understanding of creating brain-friendly environments where people can thrive is the new leadership power skill. It can help explain why your staff aren't thrilled about the latest business management

As a leader, having a basic understanding of creating brain-friendly environments where people can thrive is the new leadership power skill.

system change you want to implement. It can assist leaders in understanding what sends their employees into threat mode when receiving feedback and how leaders can use the power of language to make it a more positive process.

It makes sense to invest in self-awareness development for your staff, so they can get off auto-pilot and challenge their behavioural response and their thinking. For rural and regional leaders whose staff have been navigating difficult ongoing events like bushfires, it may explain why they aren't coming up with lots of new ideas for innovation.

It also explains why some of the more aggressive, power-driven behaviours we see on display by prominent leaders (federal parliament question time, anyone?) are not just inappropriate; they actually inhibit people's ability to do their best. If you're a leader looking for results, quality, efficiency, effectiveness and outcomes, then such behaviours will undermine what you are trying to achieve.

Well-being impacts decision-making

The well-being ladder (figure 7) demonstrates how our state of mind relates to our performance and ability to make good decisions. When we are burnt out, our brains have nothing left to give. It makes sense that our decisions aren't great, doesn't it? So why, when there is a hidden mental health epidemic in the workplace (and in our wider world), do we feel that working harder is the only way to get through? It's crazy. We're struggling, but the only solution to get out of the mud has been to press our foot harder to the accelerator. As any rural person will know, all that happens is that the wheels spin, and we end up totally bogged. Or we run out of petrol. Or we overheat the engine. None of which make progress.

As Einstein is often quoted, 'The definition of insanity is doing the same thing over and over again and expecting a different result'.

Figure 7: The relationship between well-being and decision-making

We shut down under stress

Neuroscience tells us that when we're experiencing negative emotions such as stress or when we feel unsafe or threatened (below the line in the grey area of the well-being ladder), the lower, more primitive, reptilian brain (the amygdala) is triggered and activates a threat response (fight, flight, freeze or appease) (Figure 8).

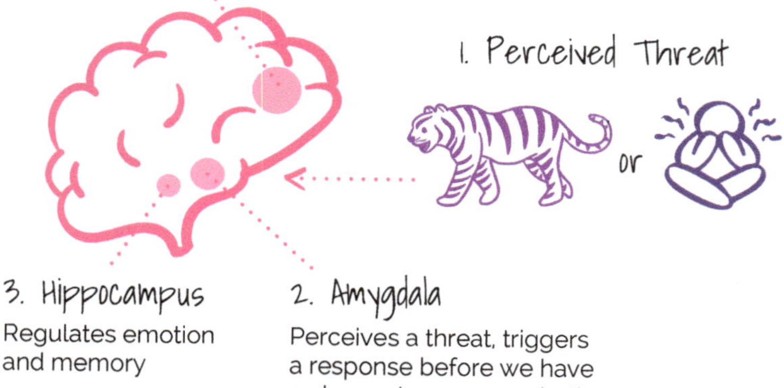

Figure 8: Your brain's response to stress

Our brains are flooded with the stress hormone cortisol; parts of our brain shut down, we are reactive and unable to perform at our best. Stress shrinks our brain networks (Figure 9). We can't retain new or call up old information. We can't think properly or listen to others. Our lens to the world narrows, and we focus on survival and ourselves. This results in lower productivity, lower innovation and lower success.

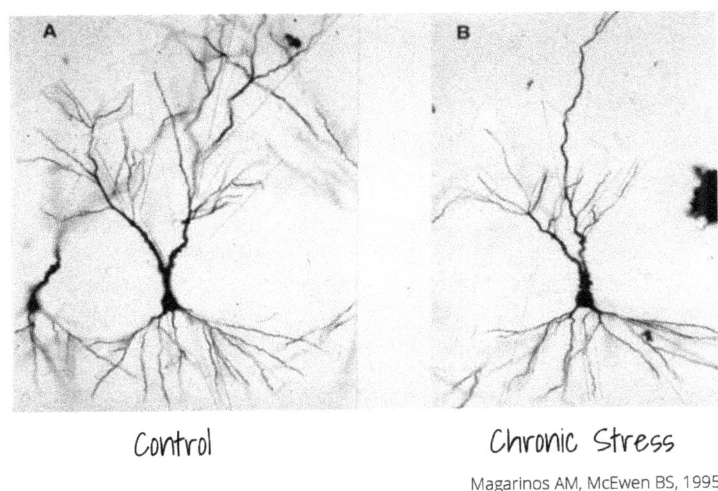

Figure 9: Stress shrinks the brain networks and can lead to neurological issues over time (McEwan & Mirsky, 2018).

Psychologist Dr Barbara Fredrickson has extensively studied the power of positivity and noted, 'Just as water lilies retract when sunlight fades, so do our minds when positivity fades' (Fredrickson B. L., 2009).

When stressed, our perceptions change, and life gets harder. A study by the University of Virginia found that if someone in a negative state of mind perceives a hill they need to climb, as thirty per cent steeper than it actually is (Achor, 2017).

When we don't feel threatened or under stress, we down-regulate cortisol and up-regulate the feel-good hormone oxytocin. Increasing oxytocin protects against stress, and when released, we feel content and calm. Our anxiety, fear and nervousness are reduced. Feelings of human bonding and trust occur. In this state, we are operating out of the pre-frontal cortex (the executive functioning part of the brain). This enables us to think clearly, listen, reason, collaborate, problem-solve, control impulses, be creative and innovative, persevere, and perform at our best. Our lens to the world widens, and we have more perspective and can connect with others.

> Increasing oxytocin protects against stress, and when released, we feel content and calm.

Organisational anthropologist Judith Glaser explains how our brain processes these trust and mistrust responses separately like this, 'Consider this simple analogy: a door guards the entrance to our inner self. When we feel trust, we readily open that door, exchanging thoughts, feelings and dreams with someone else. When we distrust someone, thinking that they are somehow a threat, we slam our door quickly and begin to defend ourselves' (Glaser J. E., 2016).

Friend or foe – how do we know?

I once had a manager called John whom I needed to speak with about a project I wanted him to support. He sat on the other side of my workstation partition, so I stood up and asked to talk with him about it. John stood too, and I launched into an excited explanation about what I saw as the benefits of this project. It was a new approach! It hadn't been done in our state before! It was leading-edge! There was such possibility! On and on I went.

Passion is one of my strengths, and I can get very animated, so I used my hands and spoke quickly and forcefully. It slowly dawned that John didn't seem to be engaging with what I was saying, so

I went even harder, and in doing so, dug myself deeper into the hole. John started to turn to the side – as though he wanted to run away. That action snapped me into helicopter view, where I could see the scene playing out.

What on earth was I thinking? John was in complete threat mode. He wasn't listening to what I was saying and just wanted to get away from me. My project had no chance unless I could re-engage and make him feel safe enough to process what I was saying.

With this awareness and knowledge, I got off auto-pilot, stopped thinking about what appealed to me about the project and started thinking about John's perspective. My tone and animated body language were freaking him out, so I slowed down my speech, spoke in a deeper tone and stopped flapping my hands.

John liked process. He was thorough and needed to know that risks were thought through and planned for. I started to use words that he would connect with – that I'd observed the approach piloted and evaluated in other states, that I had consulted the industry and they were very supportive, and that the risks were low.

His body language changed, and he started to turn back towards me. With his brain no longer in threat mode, he could consider the idea. We finished our conversation with John saying, 'That sounds like an interesting idea, Cynthia. Write me a one-pager, and I will consider it.' I did, and he eventually approved the project.

Had I remained unaware of the threat I was triggering in John, the project would never have been approved. Taking the helicopter view meant I could disrupt myself, interrupt my default way of speaking and borrow a style of communication that made John feel safe and appealed to what he valued rather than what I valued.

Because our brains decide to trust or mistrust in a millisecond, we can misinterpret the signals we receive and may see enemies instead of friends. Other people can also mistake the signals we send out. We've all encountered situations where we have the best intentions, only to have them thrown back in our face and end in conflict.

Our brains are wired to see threats, so we have a bias for noticing what is going wrong (negativity bias). It's up to us to purposefully notice the good things and be on the lookout for positive moments. With finite brain resources, paying attention to negative things leaves limited capacity to notice the positive. When we pay attention to the positive things throughout the day, our health and well-being get a huge boost (Achor, 2012). Focusing on and experiencing the positive aspects of life like joy, gratitude, love, pride, hope, amusement, inspiration, awe, serenity and curiosity builds new neural structures in the brain – so you can teach an old dog new tricks (Fredrickson B. L., 2009).

The Goldilocks effect

Another scientific theory that further supports the counter-productive nature of the continual pressure we face to keep performing at higher and higher levels is Yerkes-Dodson's Law. Psychologists Yerkes and Dodson studied the relationship between stress and performance (Fire Up Coaching, 2015). It's a bit like Goldilocks and the three bears. When Goldilocks went to taste the porridge on the kitchen table, one bowl was too cold, one was too hot, and one was just right.

When bored and disengaged, we don't secrete enough stress hormones to perform well (the porridge is too cold). When we face too much challenge, or it goes on for too long, and we're at the bottom of the well-being ladder on the rungs of overwhelm and burnout, our stress hormone levels get too high. This is called frazzle, and our performance is hampered (the porridge is too hot). When we are in the 'just right' zone of flow, we perform at our best (the porridge is just right).

Once we understand the science, I believe that organisational culture, leadership style, behaviour and choices are often counter-productive to what we say we want to achieve.

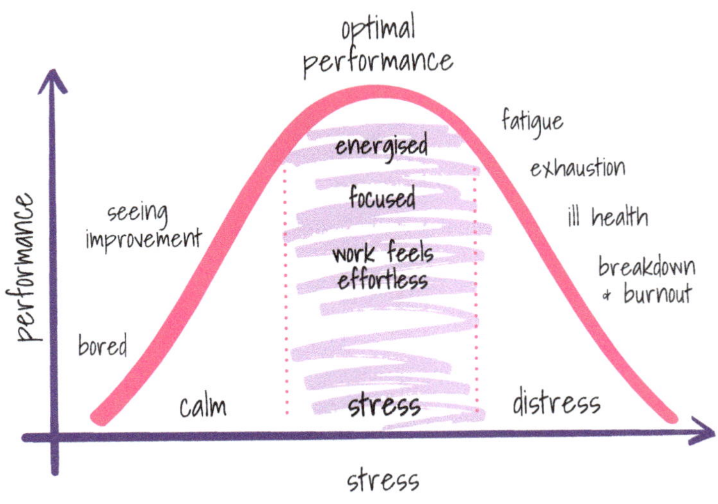

Figure 10: Yerkes Dodson's Law (Hernández, 2020)

Behaviour influences leadership

As a leader, it is helpful to understand how you can influence your people, through your own mindset and behaviour, to move up the well-being ladder from unresourceful states to more resourceful and productive states, allowing them to make better decisions. It all starts with you and your behaviour.

A range of behaviours leads others to feel threatened, including judging, needing to be right, excluding others, criticising, dictating to, being angry, withholding information, limiting others, power plays and not being clear (leading to uncertainty).

To feel safe and accepted, we need trusting environments. Trust is created when we experience behaviours of appreciating, sharing, celebrating, transparency, inclusivity, empathy, discovering, developing, co-creating and expanding (Glaser J. E., 2014).

> To attract and retain staff, create a great place to work and have thriving, productive people over the long term, smart leaders put their efforts into creating and cultivating environments of trust.

Again, this is not touchy-feely, feel-good stuff. To attract and retain staff, create a great place to work and have thriving, productive people over the long term, smart leaders put their efforts into creating and cultivating environments of trust. Focus on being self-aware and be mindful and deliberate about your behaviour and how you choose to respond to various situations and people.

The limited leader (who may be very well-intentioned) is usually on autopilot – reacting rather than responding, not choosing their behaviour, and unaware of their impact on others. They crack the whip to get short-term gains. These can lead to the over-production of stress hormones which results in burnout, stress and high turnover.

Chronic stress increases the risk of chronic disease through the actions of cortisol.

Think about the best leaders and work environments you've been in. What behaviours allowed you to flourish and be at your best? What about those that left you dreading work, feeling stressed and anxious? What about your own behaviours? Which do you show most often?

Are you up for the challenge? Becoming a cultivating person, leader and organisation takes effort. It doesn't just happen. Cultivating skills are power skills – not soft skills. Telling people what to do is easy but doesn't work in the long term if that's your only way of leading.

To lead others effectively, you must lead yourself first. Business author and speaker Tom Peters has held this mantra for more than forty years. He says, 'Hard (numbers/plans/org charts) is Soft. Soft (People/Relationships/Culture) is Hard' (Peters, 2021). Peters is a big fan of a book called ***Compassionomics*** written by two physician scientists. In the foreword to that book, Senator Corey Booker writes, 'We are often led to believe that sentiments like compassion and kindness are expressions of weakness rather than signs of strength. And we are often all too ready to give in to the false belief that meanness somehow equates to toughness and that empathy is empty of power. But the evidence in this book suggests the opposite' (Trzeciak & Mazzarelli, 2019).

Cultivating positive brain-friendly cultures is a deliberate act. Organisations can't just invest occasionally in these power skills. They are life skills that help us have better relationships with ourselves, our colleagues, clients, families and communities. Developing these skills and cultures doesn't happen through an occasional team-building workshop when a difficult situation arises.

The great news is that we can all develop better skills to foster trusting environments through our conversations. We can also regulate our behaviour when we experience a mistrust response. By observing our reactions, we can use strategies to get out of our amygdala and access the pre-frontal cortex. Taking deep breaths is one simple and effective strategy.

Reflection questions

What resonated with you in this chapter?

What insights do you have (about yourself, your leadership, your organisation/industry/community)

What could you cultivate (grow more of?)?

What could you eliminate (do less of)?

If you did this, how would your life be different?

If you did this, who else would benefit?

How would they benefit?

If you don't make a change, what are the consequences?

6

Behaviours to Eliminate vs Behaviours to Cultivate

'Before you diagnose yourself with depression or low self-esteem, first make sure that you are not, in fact, just surrounded by assholes.'

@debihope

(d.e.b., 2010)

Do you know the current state of leadership in rural Australia? What leadership behaviours dominate your rural industry, organisation or community? What go-to leadership behaviours do you rely on when expressing your leadership?

I sent a survey to my network to ask them about the old-school, dinosaur behaviours they observed in rural Australian leaders that they felt needed to be gone, never to be seen again. I also asked them to name the great rural leaders they admired, the qualities they displayed, and the leadership behaviours they wanted to see more of. All the respondents were women, and all worked in agriculture as farmers or associated service providers, educators, community engagement. I've done plenty of work with the health sector and have found their leadership experiences similar.

The sample responses below are in the survey respondents' own words (see the Appendices for a full list of responses).

Behaviours to eliminate (Get rid of)

- Authoritarian – 'My way or the highway'
- Micromanagement
- Like selecting like (no diversity)
- Exclude and undermine others
- Combative and sees others as threats
- Limited creativity – 'This is how it has always been done' culture. Not adapting or willing to adopt new ideas/tech
- Talk the talk but not often walk the walk
- Push people to their absolute limits to see just how much they can get out of them
- Put self-interest above all else – feathering their own nest
- Boys' club mentality – it's strong and should be gone

- The traditional masculine model of leadership
- Have to know everything, always needs to be right
- Lead by fear and blaming and shaming others
- Punish people for calling out poor behaviour
- Opposed to listening
- Lack of integrity
- Patriarchal
- Not living by values, or values as tokenism
- Avoid difficult conversations.

Behaviours to cultivate (Grow more of)

- Always challenge you to be your best self
- Open to suggestions and change
- Coach
- Listen to people from all walks of life – try to understand all sides of each story
- Inclusive, process-driven collaborative approach
- Honest and humble
- Never defensive or irritated when provided with feedback or recommendations to improve
- Tell the truth, no matter how difficult
- Talk the talk. Walk the walk
- Bring people together to make positive change that is inclusive of the community
- Can play the game but not the person
- Focus on building other people up, not tearing them down to make the leader look good
- Approachable, calm, listen, generous, authentic, kind, fair
- Mentor empathetically and genuinely want others to do

well. Opens doors and offers a hand up in career and profession
- Put collective outcomes well above self-interest
- Integrity, honourable and principled
- Clear about expectations
- Willing to step up and be brave
- Select women and different cultures with equal skills and abilities or even more
- Lead from within, not above, and bring others along with them
- Focus on delivering on what our industry needs rather than politicking and back-scratching.

Interestingly, the behaviours people want to see more of correspond closely with what neuroscience says make people feel safe and able to perform at their best. Those behaviours people want to eliminate lead our brains to produce more of the stress hormone cortisol and be unable to think or operate well.

Operating above or below the line

In my coaching with teams and leaders, I use a tool called Above and Below the Line to open the conversation and help define the behaviours that make a positive working environment (The Conscious Leadership Group, 2014). These define the behaviours they want to cultivate and grow, and those they want to eliminate or see less of.

What's the line? It's the line of choice. This tool says that we each have a choice in how we behave in any situation. How do you choose to act? Below the line is being a victim, blaming and shaming, refusing to take personal accountability. It includes all those behaviours in the eliminate list above. Operating above the line is where the person or team or group is taking responsibility and ownership, seeking solutions, behaving towards others respectfully, listening – all those behaviours in the cultivate list.

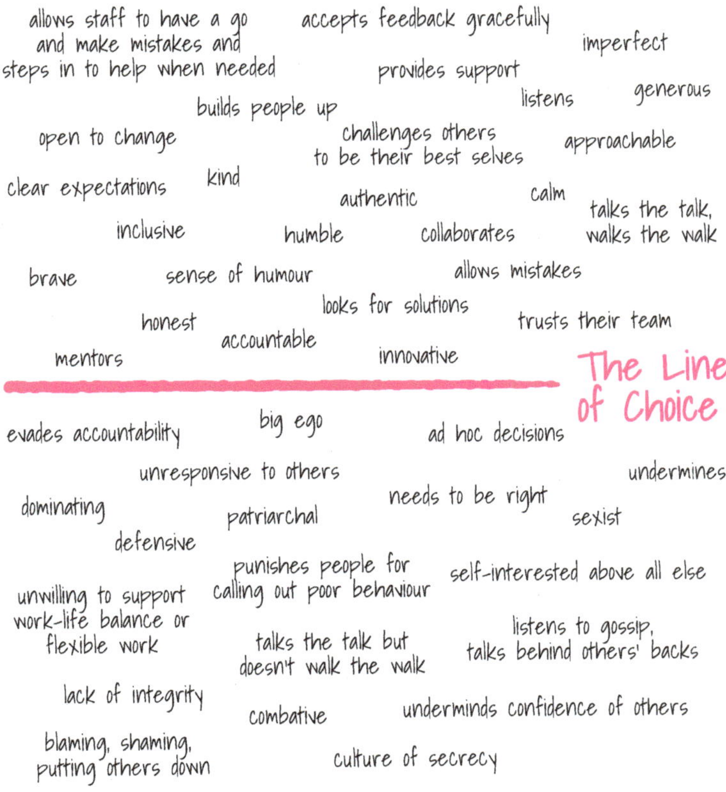

Figure 11: Leadership behaviours above and below the line

Positive environments and above the line behaviours enhance people's performance. This is confirmed in plenty of research, including the conversational intelligence work of Judith Glaser (Glaser J. E., 2014) and positive psychology research done by

> Positive environments and above the line behaviours enhance people's performance.

Shawn Achor (Achor, 2010). Negative environments where people don't feel safe, where there is no trust and where behaviours are below the line impede performance.

Research by Georgetown University's School of Business Professor Christine Porath and her colleague Christine Pearson found that 'incivility made people less motivated'. Their 2013 study of eight hundred managers across seventeen industries found how those experiencing incivility reacted. (Porath & Pearson, 2013).

- Eight per cent intentionally decreased their work effort.
- Forty-seven per cent intentionally decreased the time spent at work.
- Thirty-eight per cent intentionally decreased the quality of their work.
- Eighty per cent lost work time worrying about the incident.
- Sixty-three per cent lost work time avoiding the offender.
- Sixty-six per cent said that their performance declined.
- Seventy-eight per cent said that their commitment to the organisation declined.
- Twelve per cent said that they left their job because of the uncivil treatment.
- Twenty-five per cent admitted to taking their frustration out on customers.

These behaviours are a huge cost to organisations and industries, let alone the personal toll they take on the people at the receiving end.

You can't be what you can't see

So why are behaviours that impede performance still shown by many leaders in rural and regional Australia? One woman I spoke with worked as a counsellor and CEO in rural and regional organisations. She said that the same behaviours were rife over her twenty-five years in the sector, and many boards and committees had not changed with the times. Her explanation? 'You can't be what you don't see.'

Think about it. If most of the behaviour you are seeing in your leaders is below the line, it's not hard to imagine this is how all leaders act. When used often enough by people with a profile and tolerated or even encouraged, these behaviours become the norm or dominant way of operating. No wonder that newer people stepping up to leadership think this is how they need to behave to survive or thrive.

As my survey respondents commented, some of the leadership behaviours they didn't like involved not encouraging diversity of opinion, gender or culture and only valuing those who had traits like them.

'You can't be what you don't see.'

It's a double whammy. The leadership behaviours valued are those that got current leaders to where they are today, and younger people learn these negative behaviours from supposed role models. People who don't like this mode of operating don't put themselves forward and aren't seen as leaders because they don't display this behaviour. Current leaders don't receive feedback that their behaviours are counter-productive, and the cycle continues.

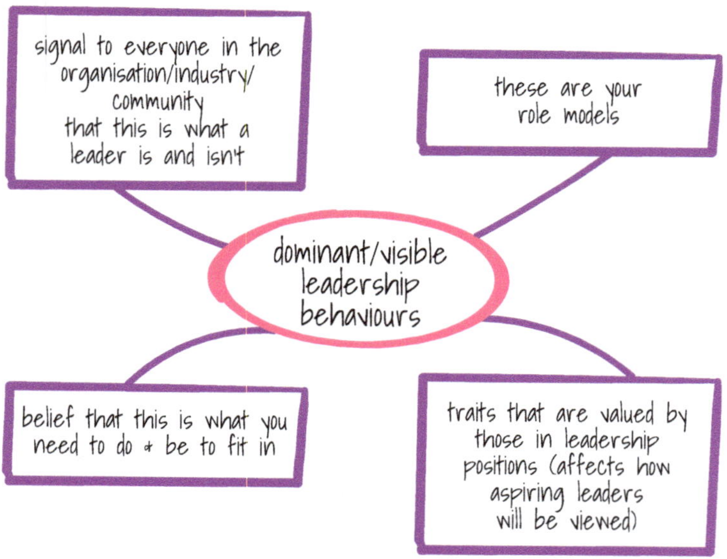

dominant cultivating behaviours

- ✔ psychological safety
- ✔ welcoming/open to all
- ✔ leadership is an activity, not a role
- ✔ diversity is sought
- ✔ a range of people apply and are encouraged to apply
- ✔ different perspectives are gained and valued
- ✔ better outcomes for industry/ organisation/community

dominant below-the-line behaviours

- ✔ not a safe environment for all
- ✔ welcoming for some, others perceived a threat
- ✔ leadership is a role, not an activity
- ✔ narrow views on what a leader is – hierachical
- ✔ like attracts like, only those that fit the dominant model are valued
- ✔ narrow perspectives are gained and valued
- ✔ poorer outcomes for industry/ organisation/community

Figure 12: The cycle of leadership

I will never forget working on an agricultural industry leadership program for emerging leaders. This group of twenty young men and women from across Australia spent much of the program talking about their vision for the industry. It was all about collaboration, working together, being positive, growing, being sustainable, supporting and encouraging each other, everyone heading in the same direction and the importance of connecting with each other, consumers and the community.

We talked about how to have respectful and tough conversations, how to navigate conflict productively and with grace, and how each could contribute to their industry in their own unique way as a leader, no matter their role. It was inspiring.

At the conclusion of the six-month program, we gathered in Canberra for the graduation ceremony. The chair of the industry board stood up to give his address. It was supposed to be about honouring the graduates and shining the spotlight on them as future leaders of the industry. Instead, he launched a vitriolic political attack on the agriculture minister (who was a guest at the event), and his speech became about point-scoring, chest-beating, shaming, belittling, negativity, blame, blokey, bully-boy tactics, us and them.

It was the absolute antithesis of the culture we had spent six months building with our group of emerging leaders. A great example of old-school leadership that should have died off years ago but for some reason persists in many organisations and industries. His speech highlighted the disconnect between the behaviour of some of our rural and regional leaders, and what people want to see.

I was involved in this annual leadership program for six years. The participants were different in each cohort, but their vision for leadership was the same. Both the women and the men wanted to be, and yearned for, cultivating leaders.

The great thing is that most people in my leadership and team programs don't want to operate below the line. They are like the young leaders above, who want to be in cultivating cultures with cultivating leaders. The feeling is universal across farmers, service providers, industry organisations, not-for-profits, government, corporate, small business, and local government.

It really hits home when they learn the above and below the line tool and concepts from Brené Brown (Brown B. , 2018), such as clearly defining what's OK and what's not OK behaviour in a team. In the absence of these conversations, there are no boundaries or guideposts for acceptable behaviour. Nothing empowers peers and others to speak up and call out poor behaviour because it's never been defined.

The following tweet came from a rural leader in my network:

> Why do #dinosaurs of our industry wear bad #governance as such a badge of honour? Feeling like I have been in the #boxingring #ignorance must be bliss
>
> 2 3 12

Figure 13: Tweet from rural leader

When people get into leadership positions and work with no operating manual, they make it up on the fly and usually fall back on what they learnt growing up. Given that many of us have not been taught this stuff by our family role models (particularly around conflict), that's not ideal. Avoiding conversations about what is and is not OK is chaotic, confusing, and lacks transparency. In its absence, the only way people learn how to behave is by watching others.

The research backs this up. Christine Porath and Christine Pearson's work on incivility found that twenty-five per cent of badly-behaved managers said they modelled their behaviour on that of their leaders who were also rude. Some leaders demonstrate behaviours people would like to eliminate because they aren't aware of an alternative way to operate. They don't know what they don't know. Porath and Pearson's research also found that many uncivil people don't recognise their behaviour as such and don't really understand what it means to be civil (Porath & Pearson, 2013).

Leadership must be fit for purpose

Albert Einstein said, 'We cannot solve our problems with the same thinking we used when we created them.' I believe that rural, regional and remote Australian people, teams, organisations, industries and communities will be much better served by a cultivating approach from their leaders. Imagine harnessing a diverse range of perspectives on solutions to the challenges facing us. What creativity and innovation would result from a more collective, collaborative approach? What about the amazing opportunities that could be recognised and realised by having people with different strengths and talents in the room? This won't happen if our leaders exclude people, don't make them welcome or operate in a culture of fear.

That's why I'm passionate about having conversations about behaviours and linking them to neuroscience so all leaders can add different skills and tools to their toolkit to be even more effective.

Having only one leadership style to draw on for all situations with all people is like having only a single golf club to play all your shots. Different situations and people require different leadership styles. This is the true art of leadership.

In a bushfire or an emergency, you want a leader who is authoritative, makes decisions and says, 'Do this now'. But if this is the only tool they've got in their bag, it's not going to make them effective. Before or after a fire, community engagement needs a consultative leadership style that involves listening to others. If you have a new employee in your business, you might need to use a mentoring technique. If you have an experienced employee, then take a coaching approach. Consultation doesn't work in the thick of a bushfire, but once the emergency has passed, 'my way or the highway' is thoroughly demotivating.

> Having only one leadership style to draw on for all situations with all people is like having only a single golf club to play all your shots.

I'm not naive enough to think that some people who use a dominating leadership style don't do it on purpose. They do it because it works for them. It helps them maintain power and to implement their agenda. So what to do?

That is where having these conversations and being clear about what is and is not OK is essential. Do it as a collective, not on your own. Find a team and back each other.

People today need cultivating leadership

A young woman called Abby spoke out about a divisive issue in her rural community. She tried to lead in a different way that saw her (and her husband and children) threatened and abused until she eventually withdrew. And as with Mel's example, this was a community she grew up in. Abby said, 'I looked around

– particularly at some of the respected older blokes in the community and thought, "If only they would say, cool down everyone, the way you are treating Abby is not OK. Let's be civil and have this debate respectfully", that it would have taken the heat out of the process. But no one said anything. They all stood back and just allowed it to happen.'

She decided that if she ever saw the same thing happening to someone else, she would speak up and support the person speaking up so they were not alone. That's being a cultivating leader.

There are many examples of cultivating leaders in rural and regional Australia too. During 2020, I interviewed some of my rural and regional clients about what leadership had looked like in the pandemic. They spoke of the importance of making people feel safe. Those who could, told staff they would keep their jobs and that their well-being and that of their families was most important. They recognised the need to create opportunities for connection and check in (rather than check on) with staff welfare.

The leaders expressed a great deal of care, support, kindness, and compassion. They demonstrated the need to understand different people's circumstances and factor that into the team and the work – for example, knowing who was living alone, who was educating children at home, whose mental health was suffering, or who had a loved one who was ill.

Many spoke about how good it was that working in a dispersed team, mostly from home, gave them more freedom to be themselves. They had their pets with them, and children interrupted meetings. They operated out of bedrooms, kitchens or home offices and dressed more casually. Their tech went wrong when they had to work through Zoom or Teams, just like everyone else. These factors humanised the leaders and put them on the same level as their teams.

One leader, Nadia, is the CEO of a rural not-for-profit. She explained that in the initial response to the pandemic, their primary concern was for the welfare and well-being of staff. She needed to respond honestly to her team's lockdown experience. They had done a lot of work around team values and behaviours before COVID hit, so trust was strong with a shared purpose that their work was even more critical during the pandemic. The team trusted that while they weren't physically in the office, they would all do their best.

Nadia set the expectation of 'Just do your best. That's all we expect'. Given different circumstances, there needed to be self-determination around what productivity was for each person. One staff member had a six-year-old with brain cancer. Another had moved in with her partner the week before they went to remote working – he lost his job, and she was working from home. A couple of her younger staff were in their first job. Other team members had children at home while others were alone. As the leader, Nadia needed to be very conscious of different factors within the team that impacted each person's productivity.

In his weekly 3-2-1 newsletter, author James Clear wrote, 'The strategies that made you successful in the past will, at some point, reach their limit. Don't let your previous choices set your future ceiling. The willingness to try new ideas allows you to keep advancing' (Clear, 2021).

I understand leadership is a tough gig that demands a lot from us. It's hard and can be lonely. It requires curiosity, constant reflection, re-evaluation and reinvention whilst still meeting KPIs and running demanding schedules. That's a lot. With recent advances in the science and understanding of leadership, there's more effective and enjoyable leadership ahead for your organisation, your employees and you.

Reflection questions

What resonated with you in this chapter?

What insights do you have about yourself, your leadership, your organisation, industry or community?

What could you cultivate (grow more of?)?

What could you eliminate (do less of?)?

If you did this, how would your life be different?

If you did this, who else would benefit?

How would they benefit?

If you don't make a change, what are the consequences?

PART TWO

A Self-Cultivated Person

'Sometimes, when you're in a dark place,
you think you've been buried,
but you've actually been planted.'

Christine Caine

(Caine, 2015)

7

'No one else is going to build the life you want for you. No one else will even be able to completely understand it. The most amazing souls will show up to cheer you on along the way, but this is your game. Make a pact to be in it with yourself for the long haul, as your own supportive friend at every step along the way.'

Tara Mohr

(Mohr, 2020)

Know your ground

Sarah is a leader in a statewide organisation who came to me for coaching after she had missed out on a senior leadership role. She was devastated as she'd received feedback from senior management that they didn't perceive her as leadership material. Her director said, 'I don't see you enough in organisational forums' and indicated that she wasn't contributing as she should be. This was in stark contrast to her team and industry peers, who greatly admired and respected her leadership qualities.

To make matters worse, the person appointed was someone Sarah knew wasn't as capable, knowledgeable or skilled as she was. Sarah hadn't seen this coming and was knocked for six. She was dedicated, caring, a subject expert in her field, proactive, positive, and now her whole sense of self – who she thought she was and where she was headed – disappeared in a moment. She was totally adrift.

She'd been sailing along, energetic and thriving, at the upper levels of the well-being ladder, when suddenly she was flung to the lower rungs, struggling, overwhelmed and stressed. A rooster one day, a feather duster the next, as the saying goes.

Stand your ground

Fast forward two years, and Sarah is now the statewide lead for a highly reputable national organisation. She is flourishing, confident, using her strengths, being strategic, looking after her well-being, and being her wonderful self.

So, what has changed?

Sarah used this setback as an opportunity for growth – the image in figure 14 shows you how she cultivated herself. Yes, all that.

As you read the rest of the book, you'll hear more about what Sarah did to cultivate herself and become a cultivating leader.

Figure 14: Sarah's self-cultivation process

What a beautiful, powerful, loving, courageous, humbling and confronting process to take yourself through. It's a great example of self-leadership and the work that it takes. Leadership starts with you.

To be self-cultivated is to lead yourself first. Be your own leader. Fully experience the seasons and the weather you are immersed in, and be OK with that. Allow, accept and love yourself, no matter what.

Contrast the cultivating process with the need to be high-performing and continually be your best self. That is too much for anyone to bear. It's an unreasonable expectation – of ourselves and others. One of the antonyms of high performance is failure. If we're not high-performing, we are failing and not good enough. Rather than high-performing, we need to give ourselves and others permission to be human.

I've seen many people who rate themselves as good leaders yet lack self-awareness and haven't done any work on themselves. They don't reflect, so they don't grow as people or as leaders. Nobody is born a leader; it is a skill to be developed. Anyone can lead – anywhere and anytime – because leadership is an activity, not a role.

Rural leaders face the challenge of being 'on' much of the time, so they are at risk of burnout. They simply must keep their batteries recharged. We recognise the need to keep our phones charged, but recharging ourselves seems more of a challenge.

Cultivating ourselves helps us stay on the upper levels of the well-being ladder and spend less time on the lower rungs. Rural leaders are role models for others in their industry and community, so looking after themselves sets a great example to others.

'I dream of never being called resilient again in my life. I'm exhausted by strength. I want support. I want softness. I want ease. I want to be amongst kin. Not patted on the back for how well I take a hit. Or for how many.' – Zandashé L'orelia Brown (Brown Z. , 2021)

Reflection questions

What resonated with you in this chapter?

What insights do you have?

What could you cultivate (grow more of)?

What could you eliminate (do less of)?

If you did this, how would your life be different?

If you did this, who else would benefit?

How would they benefit?

If you don't make a change, what are the consequences?

8

Mind Your Operating Conditions

'Everyone you meet is fighting a battle you know nothing about. Be kind. Always.'

Ian Maclaren

(Maclaren, 1897)

Choose which race are you running

It's important to remember that we operate in different conditions throughout our lives. Life can be a bit like a marathon, and it's like we are running the same race, but the conditions are continually changing for each of us. It might be foggy, so we can't find our way or bright blue skies where we feel free and happy.

Sometimes we might feel like we're in the Tough Mudder race where you're on an obstacle course climbing up ropes and crawling through mud. Some are running into a headwind while a tailwind helps others. Some of us are running in the sunshine and others in the rain.

There's also why and how we choose to undertake the race. Some are all about winning, and others care about the journey and the experience. Some do it alone, while others go as a team. Some use dirty tricks to get ahead. Others give up their place to slow down and help those who are struggling.

Some of us aren't even running in the race anymore. We've had to withdraw to rest and recover or deal with a big event. External operating conditions disrupt us, such as family ill health, having a baby, or dealing with drought or flood.

We also need to be mindful of internal operating conditions that affect our ability to run our life race. Be aware of the conditions that you're running in at any particular time, and make sure you adjust your self-cultivation strategies to respond.

Focus on running your own race, and don't compare yourself to other people. You'll be much happier.

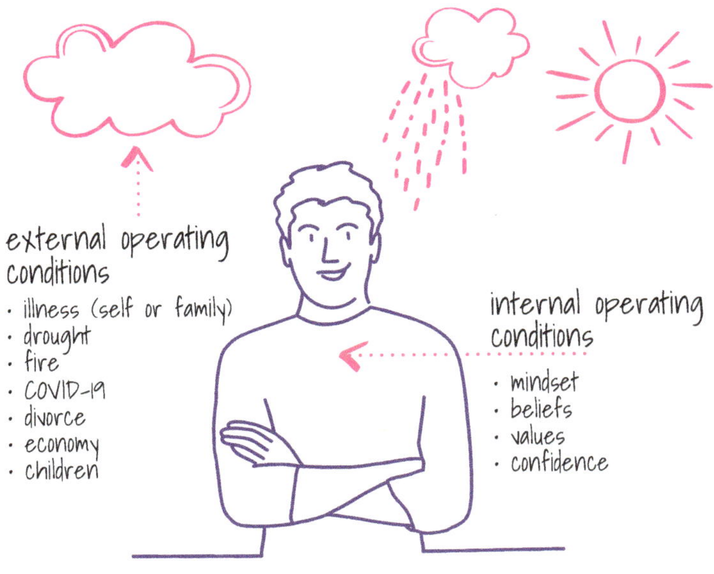

Figure 15: Mind your operating conditions

It's my vision that we can create workplaces, industries and communities where we deeply understand and allow for the conditions we are operating in. When someone isn't at their best, we get around them and give them the support they need. I want us to know ourselves and feel safe enough to ask for help, knowing we won't be judged or punished or that our careers won't be stymied. We understand that people go up and down the well-being ladder, which is part of being human. Workplaces are made up of humans, not of robots or machines. Living, breathing systems, networks and communities cultivated and nurtured with the art and skill of the gardener, rather than the technical skills of an engineer or economist measuring and optimising inputs and outputs.

Leaders with a more task-oriented approach can achieve better organisational and personal performance through a cultivating

> Workplaces are made up of humans, not of robots or machines.

approach. The opportunity to develop and grow a suite of leadership skills informed by neuroscience and positive psychology means understanding what it takes for people to flourish as humans first, with the confidence that the rest will take care of itself.

Reflection questions

What resonated with you in this chapter?

What insights do you have?

What could you cultivate (grow more of)?

What could you eliminate (do less of)?

If you did this, how would your life be different?

If you did this, who else would benefit?

How would they benefit?

If you don't make a change, what are the consequences?

9

A Model for Self-cultivation

'Knowing yourself is the beginning of all wisdom.'

Aristotle

Taking yourself off autopilot

Have you ever been driving and reached your destination, only to wonder how you got there? Recently I drove along the Hume Highway, heading to my hometown of Benalla in Northeast Victoria. It's a route I've taken thousands of times, but suddenly I got to a spot on the highway that I didn't recognise and thought, 'Where on earth am I?' It turned out I'd missed the turnoff altogether. I had not seen the sign as I was on autopilot.

> Cultivating ourselves means we have the keys to reducing conflict, blame, shame and other unproductive behaviour in the workplace and increasing personal accountability and changing culture.

So many of us are constantly operating on autopilot. It's how our brains are wired. Just as a computer has many programs and commands operating unseen in the background, so do our brains. It helps us be more efficient and expend less energy – but it comes at a cost.

One cost is that we tend to be reactive rather than responsive, which means sometimes we aren't really in control. Autopilot can turn us into robots.

What would it look like if we shifted from that state to be more intentional about how we live? Imagine the benefits to ourselves, our teams, our workplaces – less conflict, less self-sabotage, less survival mode. But how do we do it? How do we get off autopilot? The answer is to cultivate yourself.

Cultivating ourselves means we

have the keys to reducing conflict, blame, shame and other unproductive behaviour in the workplace and increasing personal accountability and changing culture.

I've identified two parts to being a self-cultivated person – one involves being aware of what is going on within you, and the other involves the actions you choose to take. These skills have helped me become more authentic and OK with myself. If we can teach these in the workplace, we will be better able to look after ourselves and create cultivating cultures for everyone.

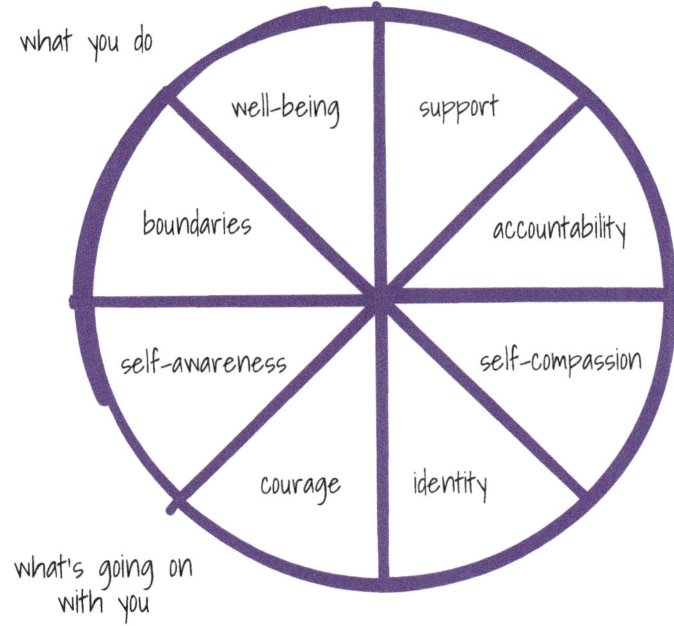

Figure 16: The wheel of self-cultivation

This model reminds us that what we put our attention on, grows. It's as the late Dr Stephen Covey reminds us in his Circle of Concern/Circle of Influence model about focusing on things we can't control. 'As long as we focus our efforts, attention and energy on those things, we accomplish nothing except to reinforce our own feelings of inadequacy and helplessness' (Covey S. R., 1989). We are reactive, acted upon by external forces and disempowered. Negative energy is generated, and we neglect those things we could actually do something about.

When you focus on cultivating yourself, you're being proactive and working on what you can do something about. This results in empowering, positive energy. You also have less brain space, time and energy to focus on things you can't do anything about.

By remembering the self-cultivation model, you can disrupt yourself and get out of reactive mode. Your thinking changes from your brain going around in circles contemplating many issues you can't do anything about to asking yourself proactive questions. What is my response here? What am I going to do? How can I show initiative in this situation? What is within my control? What sort of person do I want to be in this situation? What will my behaviour be?

What does self-cultivated mean to you? If this model doesn't work for you, consider adding different spokes to the wheel to make it reflect you.

By cultivating ourselves, we know where we are on the well-being ladder and understand we don't have to thrive all the time. We're not failing; there is nothing wrong with us if we are below the line in struggling or overwhelm. If we're self-cultivated, then hopefully, we won't get to burnout as we can intervene and be mindful that we are heading in that direction. If we are on the lower levels of the ladder, we won't spend as long there as we would have before. When we are there, we don't blame ourselves or feel unworthy or ashamed.

Reflection questions

What resonated with you in this chapter?

What insights do you have?

What could you cultivate (grow more of)?

What could you eliminate (do less of)?

If you did this, how would your life be different?

If you did this, who else would benefit?

How would they benefit?

If you don't make a change, what are the consequences?

10 Cultivating Self-awareness

'Until you make the unconscious conscious, it will direct your life, and you will call it fate.'

Carl Jung

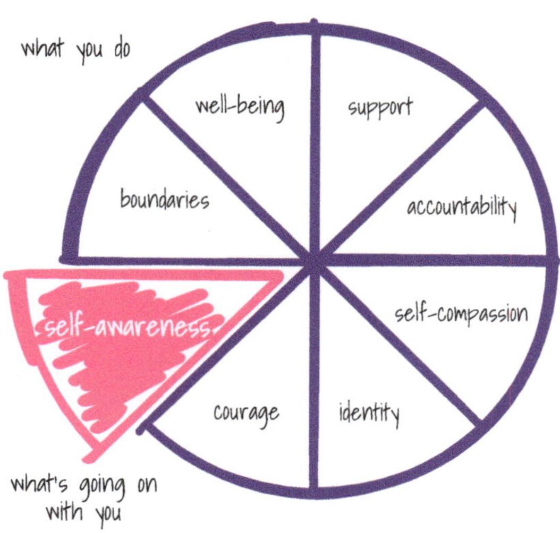

Figure 17: A self-cultivated leader develops their self-awareness

Underestimating yourself

'I'm really bad at public speaking.' 'I'm warning you, I'm going to be absolutely terrible.' 'I just don't think I can do this.' 'Public speaking's just not something I'm good at.' 'I'm fine talking one-on-one, but the minute I get up in front of a group, my mind goes blank.' These comments came from participants at an emerging leaders' program I was facilitating.

One of my roles was to observe each person as they delivered a two-minute presentation about who they were and why they were passionate about their industry. I provided feedback on what they did well and how they could raise the bar for next time.

As they prepared their content, I chatted to individuals about how they were going. Of the fifteen participants, seven quietly shared their fears that they were hopeless at public speaking.

I braced myself to sit through excruciating presentations and wondered how I would find positive feedback to share.

But you know what? They were great! Sure, there were nerves and stumbles here and there, but no disasters and some terrific performances.

For some people, just delivering the speech was enough to change their self-awareness. For others who had doubts about how they performed, the feedback they received gave them new awareness. They did have the ability to deliver a public presentation well and professionally. In fact, some of the most terrified participants were so buoyed that they volunteered to present at an industry dinner that night.

Someone highly competent can massively underestimate their talent. They assume others operate at the same level, so they think their own ability is nothing special. Most of my coaching clients fall into this category. I am constantly amazed at how many people have no idea how fabulous and unique they are. On the other hand, most of us know people who think they are far more skilled than they actually are. This is known as the Dunning-Kruger effect, where the less competent people are, the more they overestimate their abilities.

See yourself as others see you?

So what is going on? In my experience, people's self-perception can be totally out of whack with how others see them. Organisational psychologist and researcher Dr Tasha Eurich and her team found that we're not very good at self-awareness. Their five-year study involved ten separate investigations with almost five thousand participants. It revealed that ninety-five per cent of people think they're self-aware, but only ten to fifteen per cent really are.

> Dr Eurich found that having unaware team members can cut a team's chances of success in half.

We're all bumbling around in our lives, thinking we know what's going on, but most of us have no idea! There's plenty of opportunity for growth here.

Dr Eurich defined self-awareness in two parts.

Internal self-awareness represents how clearly we see our values, passions, aspirations, fit with our environment, reactions (including thoughts, feelings, behaviours, strengths, and weaknesses) and our impact on others. External self-awareness is our understanding of how other people view us in these terms (Eurich, 2017).

Just because you are good at one type of self-awareness doesn't mean that you're good at the other.

Dr Eurich found that having unaware team members can cut a team's chances of success in half. Other consequences of working with such colleagues include increased stress, increased conflict, decreased team cohesion, decreased motivation, and a greater likelihood of leaving one's job. A 2012 study showed that seventy-nine per cent of employees had a skill that they counted among their strengths, and that other co-workers saw as a weakness (Orr, 2012).

Leaders need to be particularly focused on self-awareness. Dr Eurich's research, described above, also found that senior executives are generally less self-aware than frontline and mid-level leaders. There's an inverse relationship between power and self-awareness.

A key component of self-awareness is identifying our blind spots.

We all have blind spots that, if we don't uncover and take action on, can end up derailing our relationships with others and, ultimately, our careers.

Uncover your blind spots

What exactly is a blind spot? It's where our perception of ourselves doesn't match others' perceptions of us. It can be a skill we overrate or underrate in ourselves. It can be a personal behaviour or trait that we don't see. It can also be in our conversations where we assume others see what we see, feel what we feel and think what we think.

The takeaway is that organisations, teams and individuals have plenty of opportunities for improvement in increased self-awareness and uncovering blind spots.

If we don't have the courage or the tools to explore and reveal our blind spots, the consequences can be enormous for our careers and costly for the organisation. I've worked with many coaching clients who were blind-sided, personally and professionally, by the sudden derailment of their careers. Their confidence has been shot, reputations damaged, motivation lost, performance impeded, and trust eroded. They've left jobs, taken sick leave or experienced presenteeism (where they are physically at work but not performing well). At times the reasons are more about the organisation's culture, but some have discovered that the derailment is due to a blind spot. Usually, it's one they've not received feedback on until it's almost too late.

I was working with a team to improve self-awareness and build trust. In one activity, pairs were invited to practice having courageous conversations. I observed two young men – Tom spoke, and Antonio received the feedback. Antonio then provided Tom with feedback on how he experienced the conversation.

'Umm, I found it a bit angry actually and felt a bit uncomfortable,' said Antonio. Tom was blown away. 'I had no idea!' he said. 'I felt really uncomfortable about talking, so I just said it as quickly as I could to get it over and done with.'

Tom was uncomfortable and delivered his part of the conversation awkwardly, which the receiver, Antonio, experienced as somewhat aggressive. In a real-life situation, this could have led to major misunderstandings and further tension. Tom was so focused on himself and getting the conversation over and done that he forgot about how the receiver might feel. He was totally unaware that his discomfort came across as aggressive. Antonio let him know how he felt because there was trust between them, and the activity was in a safe environment. Tom took a deep breath, calmed down and delivered the feedback again in a much more productive way.

Building self-awareness

How often does this happen to us?

As leaders, we have an obligation to support our teams to give and receive feedback in a safe and constructive environment throughout our people's careers. We need to nip things in the bud. If we dare to explore and uncover our blind spots, this helps create a positive culture of curiosity, discovery and continuous learning rather than blame and shame.

Everything about being a self-cultivated person starts with building self-awareness. It opens the door to all the other parts of the wheel of self-cultivation. There's a certain amount of humility associated with being self-aware. That means recognising that we can't possibly know all the answers and that there is always an opportunity for growth. Self-awareness requires us to do the deep inner work on ourselves, and for leaders, it's hard to lead others if you don't know how to conduct yourself.

Interestingly, many leaders are adept at prioritising key performance indicators and analysing the effect of this input on that output but don't feel the need to look at themselves. Many below-the-line leadership behaviours identified by my survey respondents are the direct result of leaders not being self-aware. It's a learnable skill, and we need to encourage this practice for ourselves and our people. If you're not self-aware, then you can't change, grow, develop or adapt. And yet, that is what our complex world and our workplaces are crying out for.

As leaders, we have an obligation to support our teams to give and receive feedback in a safe and constructive environment throughout our people's careers.

What did Sarah do?

Through her experience of missing out on the job, Sarah discovered that she had some work to do on both elements of self-awareness.

She discovered some unconscious beliefs that had been holding her back and directed her behaviour in ways that weren't serving her. Once those beliefs became conscious, she could make deliberate decisions instead of being on auto-pilot.

Sarah also had some blind spots in the second element of self-awareness – how others perceived her – specifically people in the senior leadership team in her organisation. She received feedback from a colleague who said, 'When you speak, I lean in'. Sarah commented, 'I felt so great hearing that from her, as she is so respected. I realised I had been holding back from speaking up because I kept second-guessing myself by thinking, "Is what I am going to say adding value?" I've realised that providing a different perspective is where I add value. My thinking is considered. When I talk, it is coming from a place of curiosity, not ego. I need to own my skills. I now understand my power, and I am now having conversations in the executive meetings that I wouldn't have had before.'

By becoming more self-aware, Sarah was able to identify strategies that supported her growth and development. One of these strategies was not to ask permission to be at specific meetings but simply to put herself at the table when her skills were needed and be confident that she belonged there and was adding value.

Reflection questions

What resonated with you in this chapter?

What insights do you have?

What could you cultivate (grow more of)?

What could you eliminate (do less of)?

If you did this, how would your life be different?

If you did this, who else would benefit?

How would they benefit?

If you don't make a change, what are the consequences?

11

Cultivating Courage

'Our deepest fear is not that we are inadequate. Our deepest fear is that we are powerful beyond measure. It is our light, not our darkness that most frightens us. We ask ourselves, who am I to be brilliant, gorgeous, talented, fabulous? Actually, who are you not to be? You are a child of God. Your playing small does not serve the world. There is nothing enlightened about shrinking so that other people won't feel insecure around you. We are all meant to shine, as children do.'

Marianne Williamson

(Williamson, 1996)

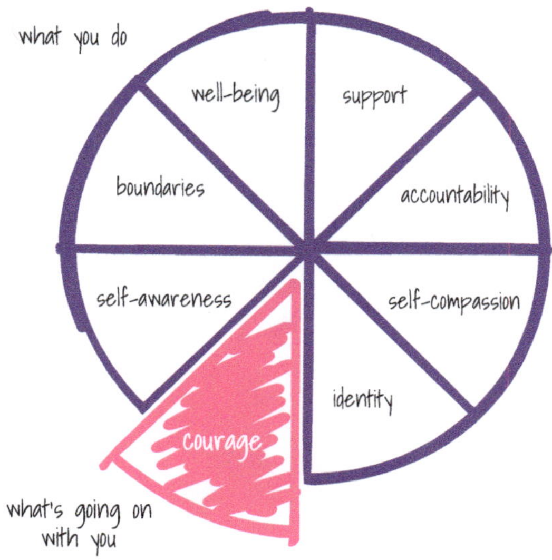

Figure 18: A self-cultivated leader practices courage

Courage unlocks us

If self-awareness is the door that allows access to all the other parts of the self-cultivated wheel, courage is the key that unlocks the door.

The word courage comes from the French word ***coeur***, which means the heart. In an interview, the director of the London School of Economics, Minouche Shafik, said, 'In the past, jobs were about muscles, now they're about brains, but in the future, they'll be about the heart' (Elkanne, 2018).

As a former economist (my first job was as an agricultural economist), I know that when economists start talking about the importance of the heart in business, things are shifting in how we view the world of work.

In an increasingly technological world where artificial intelligence is on the rise, our human skills and heart intelligence will be our competitive advantage, more necessary than ever to underpin our decision-making.

It's interesting to consider the different elements of courage. It's not just one-dimensional. Authors Jennifer Armstrong and Lisa Dungate identify six types of courage (Armstrong & Dungate, 2011).

- Physical: To keep going with resiliency, balance and awareness despite fear of physical harm
- Emotional: To allow ourselves to feel the full spectrum of human emotions
- Spiritual: To live with purpose and meaning and face up to spiritual questions that may be uncomfortable, a threat to your own identity as a spiritual person, or undermine your own spiritual beliefs
- Moral: The courage to stand up for your convictions and do the right thing despite the sense that it may end badly for you or is uncomfortable or unpopular
- Intellectual: The willingness to learn, relearn and unlearn and expand our horizons
- Social: The courage to be yourself unapologetically and expose yourself to social situations where you may be vulnerable to embarrassment, ridicule, or discomfort.

In rural Australia, we are very comfortable with acts of physical courage. Being a self-cultivating person is broadening our understanding of courage to embrace the other five types of courage.

It takes great courage to reflect and uncover our uncomfortable blind spots. It takes courage to have an honest conversation with someone. It takes courage to be vulnerable and authentic and not wear a mask or be someone you think you need to be. To speak up against the tide and say that particular behaviour is not OK. To sit with complex feelings, connect with them and deal with them. To let go of the need to be right all the time and accept there will be things you don't know that you can learn from others.

People who can't lead or connect courageously with their hearts are missing out. Not being fully expressed as humans can lead to unhappiness, lack of fulfilment, resentment, shame, anger and emotional pain. 'It takes courage to grow up and become who you really are,' wrote E.E. Cummings (Popova, 2015). Having courage leads to growth. It's feeling afraid and taking action despite this. Leading with the heart is a whole other skill set.

> It takes great courage to reflect and uncover our uncomfortable blind spots.

It's easier not to lead with the heart; it's less complicated. When you're not courageous, it's easier to be below the line, point the finger, blame, shame and not take responsibility. You don't want to sit with discomfort or feel emotional pain, so you don't listen or connect with people. You keep everything about the task and KPIs and productive units because that's easier than needing to factor in the human side.

With my colleague, Louise Thomson, I ran a series of webinars called 'Well-being Wednesday'. They involved interviews with rural women from across Australia about their experience of well-being, what it meant, their struggles with it and what they had learnt. The aim was to support our network during the lockdown challenges, connect people, and have honest conversations to inspire each other.

The women we interviewed were brave. Many had never spoken publicly before and asked, 'Why would you want to interview me?' Every woman felt the fear of speaking to an unknown group of people, and every single one stepped up and did it anyway because it would be of help and service to others. All of them were fabulous. They were vulnerable, generous, honest, open and spoke from the heart. The conversations generated between our speakers and the attendees opened up many new possibilities. We received feedback that these interviews were a lifeline for many during a tough time. Without courage, they would not have happened.

How would your life be different if you allowed yourself to be courageous in all its forms? Being courageous provides the freedom to be me without the burden of wearing a mask or hiding who I am. It's enabled me to make mistakes, learn from them and grow. Even when it's hard, I know that being courageous permits other people to be courageous as well. Imagine what our teams, organisations, industries and communities could be like if we all exercised our courage muscle more often?

What did Sarah do?

Sarah showed emotional courage in allowing herself to fully feel the disappointment of not getting the role she had gone for. She sat with the anger and resentment and then took responsibility and looked at how she could turn the situation around. Sarah showed intellectual courage by wanting to learn and grow from the experience. She showed social courage in seeking feedback from others in her network by inviting feedback.

About a year after this experience, Sarah phoned to tell me she had been offered a six-week secondment at a national organisation, taking on a role that would be a huge challenge and a big step up for her. She wanted my perspective on whether she should take it. I asked her what she would tell someone who asked her the same question? Without hesitation, she said, 'I would tell them to take it.' 'Well then!' I said. And with that, she took a risk and stepped up. It ended up being one of the best career moves she had ever made. That's courage.

Reflection questions

What resonated with you in this chapter?

What insights do you have?

What could you cultivate (grow more of)?

What could you eliminate (do less of)?

If you did this, how would your life be different?

If you did this, who else would benefit?

How would they benefit?

If you don't make a change, what are the consequences?

12

Cultivating Support

'There's a we in well-being –
you don't have to do it on your own.'

Cynthia Mahoney

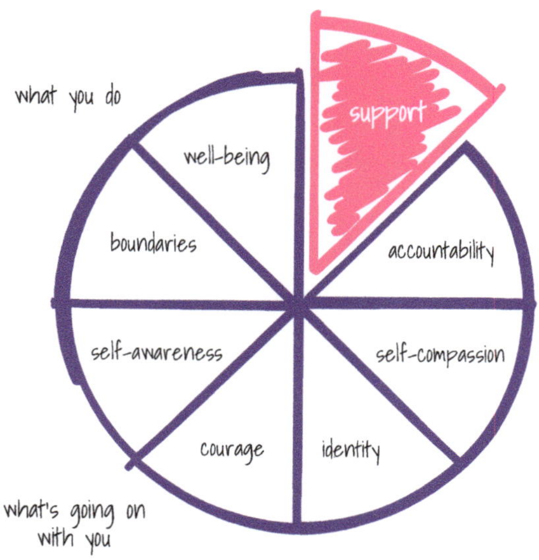

Figure 19: A self-cultivated leader gets support

Finding connection

The ABC's 7.30 program featured a story about the 6Bs – where groups of rural men come together to support each other and talk about general health and well-being. What are the 6Bs? Barbecue, bonfire, blokes, beers, bonding and bullshit. Farming can be a very lonely business, and with increased mechanisation and bigger farms, many farmers can spend most of each day on their own. This isn't just about farming; as I've noted before, leadership itself can be a lonely job. Even when others surround you, it can be hard to know whom you can trust or confide in and where to get support.

The 6Bs story featured seventy men (some had travelled more than 700km to be there) gathered at Mullewa, five hours north of Perth in Western Australia. Owen Catto from Regional Men's

Health said, 'Blokes talking through groups, feeling safe and connected, is how we're going to empower individuals and communities to talk about it and say, "Mate, that's alright, you're not the only one". Blokes need to realise that we're not alone and give each other permission to talk about stuff. When we realise that we are not the only one and that it's safe to talk about it, then we will spill our guts and talk about stuff that really matters to us' (Lewis, 2021).

After more than twenty-five years as a facilitator working with rural industries and communities, I can attest to the power of bringing people together to talk honestly about what's going on in their lives, sharing their experiences, stories and challenges, and realising that they are not on their own. I've facilitated hundreds of workshops where amazing conversations have happened, connections are made, ideas shared, and people inspired to make positive changes in their lives.

Positive social interactions stimulate changes in hormones that affect nearly every system in the body.

As human beings, we are hard-wired to connect, and we have a fundamental need to belong. It's a product of evolution, where we could not survive alone, so we depended upon and lived in cooperative societies. Mark Leary, PhD, is a professor of psychology and neuroscience at Duke University. He says, 'A solitary human being could not have survived during the six million years of human evolution while we were living out there on the African savannah' (Weir, 2012).

Positive social interactions stimulate changes in hormones that affect nearly every system in the body. Low social support is a damaging as high blood pressure, while high levels of social support are as beneficial as regular exercise. Social connection boosts your health just as much as quitting smoking.

Research by Shawn Achor found that the degree of social support people provided was even more important to sustained happiness and engagement than receiving support from others. His study found that the 'social support providers' – those people who picked up slack for others, invited coworkers to lunch, and organised office activities – were not only ten times more likely to be engaged at work than those who kept to themselves; they were forty per cent more likely to get a promotion' (Achor, 2012). So, connection with others led to increased personal happiness and increased performance.

No wonder that the 6Bs are making such a difference to rural men.

Imagine if we each built a team of people around us who knew what greatness we had inside. People who would be there through the highs and lows, and supported us to be the best we could be. How powerful that could be! What could we achieve?

As a facilitator of leadership programs, I've been fortunate to hear the wisdom of many people, all successful in their own way, with their strengths, talents and learnings about their leadership journey. One common theme is that they don't do it on their own. They surround themselves with people who have different strengths. They have all had mentors who challenged them, raised the bar for them, shared their wisdom and offered support.

My tip? Think about your network strategically and realise you don't have to do it on your own.

Imagine you are the CEO of 'You Inc'. Who would you want on your management board? Or perhaps think of yourself as a professional athlete. Who would you want in your support crew?

It's also important to remember that your network is not a one-way street. You also play an important role for many people in your network.

What did Sarah do?

Sarah's experience at work led me to become her coach. As part of Sarah's support crew, I listened, asked questions, and challenged her. We audited her network during a session and identified that she didn't have any mentors. Sarah thought about this carefully and identified someone from her past that she valued and respected. She made contact and caught up with them to get their advice and perspective on what had happened to her, how she was regarded in the wider industry and what she could do to position herself to move to the next level. Meeting with this mentor gave her some good ideas about getting her career back on track.

Sarah also identified two people in her organisation who were good at influencing upwards and asked them for advice and strategies.

She realised that she had become narrow in her role and wasn't on many cross-functional committees. Her director had told her, 'I don't see you present at things enough'. So she joined two workplace committees and advocated for her team to lead a high-profile project.

Sarah then took on a six-week secondment to another organisation. That exposed her to different state and national networks, enhanced her reputation and eventually led to her employment with that organisation.

Reflection questions

What resonated with you in this chapter?

What insights do you have?

What could you cultivate (grow more of)?

What could you eliminate (do less of)?

If you did this, how would your life be different?

If you did this, who else would benefit?

How would they benefit?

If you don't make a change, what are the consequences?

'Daring to set boundaries is about having the courage to love ourselves, even when we risk disappointing others.'

Brené Brown

(Brown B, 2018)

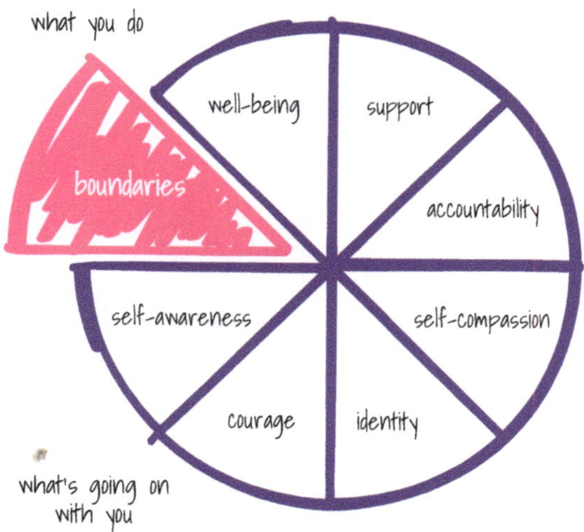

Figure 20: A self-cultivated leader identifies and protects their boundaries

Setting your non-negotiables

I take much inspiration from the people I work with who make positive changes and cultivate themselves. Liz, one of my coaching clients, transformed her life and well-being by using a simple technique to protect her boundaries. I've shared her process in many workshops, and her story has inspired others to adopt this approach with great results.

Let's hear from Liz.

'I'm a full-time dairy farmer, plus I was on the board of a Catchment Management Authority, a regional industry board, a national government advisory group, and a national industry group and I was going to Canberra quite often. It was frantic. I would look at my diary and work out where I would be for the week, how many planes I was going to catch, and how many board papers I had to read. My bag was permanently packed and ready to go – it was ridiculous. At the same time, our milk company fell over, so it was full-on.

'All of those things happened at the same time, and it was really hard. There was a big trigger for me in Canberra when I felt that no one was listening. It was so hard, and I thought that's it, that is enough, I can't keep doing this. And thankfully, at that time, I had a couple of trusted friends, and I worked through it with them.

'I decided to pull back from everything, make myself stronger and find out the authentic me. Not the person that had to be a guru on water, not the person that had to represent the dairy industry and continually be positive. Not that person, but who am I? What are my core values? What do I believe in? What are my truths? It was hard, but it was the very best thing I've ever done.

'I am now able to determine if a decision is in line with my values. This is really important, and I've worked hard on identifying what is important and where I am negotiable.

'I found it hard to set boundaries and say no until I worked out a little strategy to help. Now, if someone asks me to do something, I just say, "Can I just get back to you about that?" It doesn't offend anybody, and it's not automatically going yes or no. "Let me get back to you" gives me space and time to make a mindful decision.

'In the past, I've often been guilty when a great opportunity has come up, and I say, "Yeah, yeah, yeah, that's great." And then I think, "Oh, I'm not really sure how I'm going to fit that in my day."

'"Let me get back to you" is great, and I can highly recommend it as an answer of choice.'

Disrupting your default behaviour

One valuable skill that many women haven't developed well is giving voice to and looking after our boundaries. The default response for many (me included) is to say yes when asked to do something. And then what happens? We agree, then go away and realise that we didn't want to do that thing and then feel resentful and cheesed off.

Often we turn our resentment towards the person who asked us and take it out on them in passive-aggressive ways. We get overloaded and find we are doing a whole heap of things we don't want to do. And then we don't have time for the things that are important to us. Often this involves our well-being and self-care.

Guess what? Other people aren't mind-readers. Unless we tell them what is OK and what is not, how will they know?

So why do we do this? There are several reasons.

Social conditioning. This is particularly prevalent in women conditioned to look after others. It has become so ingrained that we think it's selfish to put ourselves first and look after ourselves. We also have 'nice lady syndrome' where we feel the need to please others to be loved and accepted. What a load of rubbish! Let's break free from that constraint.

Glennon Doyle has written a book with the fabulous title of ***Untamed – Stop Pleasing and Start Living*** (Doyle, 2020). In it, she writes, 'We do not honour our own bodies, curiosity, hunger, judgement, experience, or ambition. Women who are best at this disappearing act earn the highest praise: She is so selfless. Can you imagine? The epitome of womanhood is to lose oneself completely.'

Since childhood, we've learned to ask for permission. Afraid of rejection, disapproval and judgement, we limit our dreams and expectations, make ourselves small and give our power away.

We're not even aware we do it. I love Brené Brown's view that whenever we feel resentful towards someone, it's usually because we haven't stood up for one of our boundaries. And then, instead of taking responsibility for that ourselves, we blame the other person. Resentment is a red flag that signals boundaries have been overstepped (Brown B. , 2018).

We haven't spent time examining and defining what is most important to us. Do you know your non-negotiables? Are you clear on your values? Have you made time for a conversation with someone about your needs?

Many of us don't do this inner work and reflection. We haven't defined what we need or want, so it's easier to say yes to others. That fills up the space, and then we believe we don't have time for ourselves. We end up running around like headless chooks, exhausted and resentful. When people ask how we are, we say, 'busy'. Our identities are tied up in what we do. If we took time to stop and reflect, who would we be?

It's helpful to remember that when you say yes to something, you are saying no to something else.

It's helpful to remember that when you say yes to something, you are saying no to something else. And the reverse is also true. Getting clear on the consequences of what we are saying 'yes' and 'no' to is important in helping define boundaries. We demonstrate our priorities by what we spend our time doing.

We're afraid of offending people. The thing is, people might not like it when you start voicing your boundaries because your yes to whatever they ask has worked well for them. So they might push back. Being clear on what is important to you helps here. You are responsible for your own feelings and reactions, not the reactions and feelings of others. You will never please everyone, and not everyone will like you. Taking a leaf out of Taylor Swift's *Shake It Off* playbook is helpful:

> 'Cause the players gonna play, play, play, play, play
> And the haters gonna hate, hate, hate, hate, hate
> Baby, I'm just gonna shake, shake, shake, shake, shake
> I shake it off, I shake it off (Whoo-hoo-hoo)
> (Swift, Martin, & Shellback, 1989).

We don't know how to voice it. The most common issue people approach me about is how to have difficult conversations. Many are deeply uncomfortable about having them. Some helpful tools outline how to have courageous conversations and set out a structure to follow. (DS Psychology, 2017) (Brown B., 2021) (The Creating WE Institute, 2021). I've found that once people learn and practice how to frame a conversation, they gain more confidence in raising tricky issues.

We have unconscious rules we've set for ourselves. Have you ever thought, 'Oh, I could never do or say that? Or ask for that? Or be that? Or have, deserve, expect that, or say yes to that?' The rules – conscious and unconscious – that drive our behaviour and our decisions seem perfectly legitimate until we become aware and challenge them. These internal rules are called generalisations.

Sometimes the best thing we can do for our well-being is to get out of our own way. Stop holding back and start giving ourselves permission rather than looking to someone else to do so. That puts the ball firmly back in our court to take responsibility and be accountable.

> Sometimes the best thing we can do for our well-being is to get out of our own way.

There are too few people doing too

much in many rural communities, and volunteer fatigue is rife. From my well-being workshops, I know that some people find it hard to say no and feel things will fall apart without them. However, being resentful or burnt-out isn't great for you or your community.

> When we're self-cultivated, we take time to reflect on and define our boundaries.

When we're self-cultivated, we take time to reflect on and define our boundaries. We have clarity and understand what we are agreeing to and what we are turning down. By acting from a place of integrity and clearly understanding our values and what is important, we have more courage, confidence and assertiveness to let others know when our boundaries are crossed. Maintaining boundaries is an act of self-love, self-care and compassion. It's a great gift to ourselves and those around us.

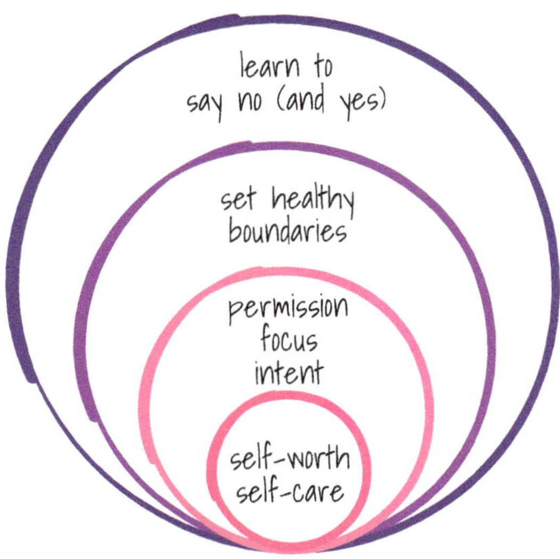

Figure 21: How boundaries support self-care

What did Sarah do?

Sarah recognised that putting boundaries around her work and home life was crucial to her well-being. I asked her to consider what her ideal job would look like. She wanted to put limits on how she worked and her work-life arrangements. Sarah also identified that she needed to express these to other people, including her team, and ask for their support in holding her accountable.

I asked what she thought when other people put boundaries in place? She said she admired their strength in saying no and being clear about that. She never held it against them. We explored why it was different for her and why she didn't permit herself to say no. She realised she was running an unconscious belief that it wasn't OK for her to set boundaries because she wasn't clear on what was important to her.

Once she could clearly define what mattered and what she needed for self-care and well-being, Sarah worked out a plan that included putting boundaries around when she would switch off from work. She also asked her family and team for support in doing this. Her final step in the process was to be aware of prioritising her well-being when saying no (or yes). This gave her more confidence and the ability to stand up for her boundaries.

Reflection questions

What resonated with you in this chapter?

What insights do you have?

What could you cultivate (grow more of)?

What could you eliminate (do less of)?

If you did this, how would your life be different?

If you did this, who else would benefit?

How would they benefit?

If you don't make a change, what are the consequences?

14

Cultivating Compassion

'Having compassion starts and ends with having compassion for all those unwanted parts of ourselves, all those imperfections that we don't even want to look at. Compassion isn't some kind of self-improvement project or ideal that we're trying to live up to.'

Pema Chödrön

(Chödrön, 2000)

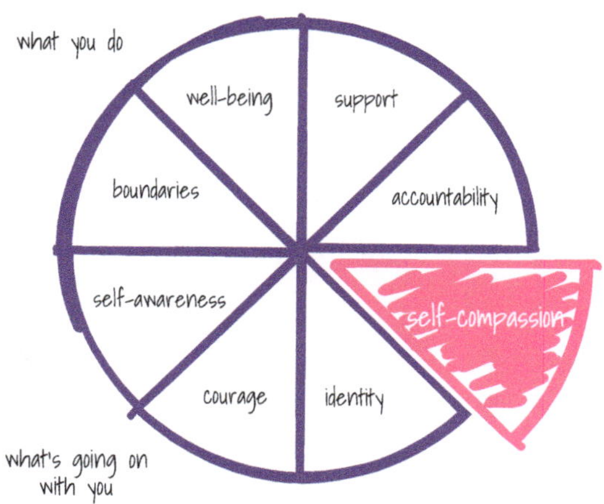

Figure 22: A self-cultivated leader practices compassion

Talking to ourselves

Do you speak to other people the same way you talk to yourself? Are you aware of what your inner voices are saying? I don't know about you, but sometimes I'm not very kind to myself. Little voices chatter away in my head, saying, 'You should do this. You shouldn't do that. Ooh, look at her over there. She's got a really good life. Why can't you be more like her? You're too much of this and not enough of that'. On and on it goes.

We can be extremely self-critical, judging ourselves in ways that we don't judge others and holding ourselves to impossibly high standards. We feel we need to know everything and that there's something wrong with us if we don't. Would you speak to your worst enemy the way you speak to yourself at times? It's no way to live.

At times that lack of self-compassion means we are hard on others. We judge, jump to conclusions, blame, shame and don't listen.

The literal meaning of compassion is to suffer together. It's our ability to understand another person's emotional state as well as our own. Compassion motivates us to help others and ease their suffering (Newport Academy, 2018). I think many of us could practice greater self-compassion to ease our own suffering.

A self-cultivated person is their own best friend and accepts themselves, warts and all. It helps to weather the ups and downs of life, knowing that whatever happens, we are enough, we are worthy, and we accept ourselves.

A self-cultivated person is their own best friend and accepts themselves, warts and all.

If we bring cultivation to our way of being, we think and act in a gentler, kinder, more compassionate, sustainable, and realistic way. The attitude of high performance can end up being a rod for our own backs when self-talk says, 'I must be better, I am not enough, I need to do more'. It's a scarcity mentality, where cultivate is a mindset of abundance – I am enough, just as I am.

Self-compassion is a generous practice. Dr Kristen Neff is a pioneer in the field of self-compassion. She writes, 'Most people find that when they're absorbed in self-judgement, they have little bandwidth left over to think about anything other than their inadequate, worthless selves. However, when we can be kind and nurturing to ourselves, many of our emotional needs are met, leaving us in a better position to focus on others' (Neff, 2015).

Compassion requires us to get out of our heads and into our hearts. A cultivating person allows themselves and others to be human, fail, make mistakes, and be enough.

Imagine how different our workplaces would be if we could be real. Accepting ourselves and being self-compassionate allows us to remove the mask and show up as we are. Not to perform or pretend. It's OK to fail; it's OK not to get it right; you don't need to be perfect.

The thought of high-performing and needing to be more sets my body into a clenching, tightening state of tension. Cultivating and self-compassion make me feel like I'm taking a deep breath and releasing the tension. It's surrender, acceptance and being in a relaxed state. It's letting go and accepting energy rather than forcing it. It's such a relief.

Barriers to compassion

Self-talk is one of the most significant barriers to self-compassion. Unless we're conscious of our self-talk and find ways to interrupt it, it can be destructive and keep us stuck in old patterns of behaviour that no longer serve us. Remember, your thoughts are just thoughts, they aren't reality, and you don't have to believe them. We can choose not to listen to our self-talk, but first, we must be aware of it.

The other major barrier to self-compassion is comparisonitis – looking at everyone else, comparing yourself to them and coming up short every time. One of my clients is a super-talented, insightful, wise, emotionally intelligent and courageous leader who has had some time out of the workforce raising her children. She returned in a part-time role. On a recent Zoom call, she found herself looking at her team and thinking, 'What on earth am I doing here? They are all so great. I'm in awe of them. I'm just not good enough'.

All this, from a woman who led a statewide team in a male-dominated agricultural industry at the age of thirty and was highly respected by all who knew her.

A self-cultivated individual looks for ways to extend compassion to others.

I'm often on Twitter, which can be a very negative environment. If you want to see a whole lot of triggered people reacting rather than mindfully responding, then this is the place to go. There can be plenty of judgement, anger, shaming, abusing, criticising, blaming and below the line behaviour.

I often have to stop myself from tweeting a critical comment (although I did call someone a goose the other day – self-compassion reminds me that I'm human and sometimes not my best self!). Instead, I try not to respond to posts that trigger me. Or if something has and I'm tempted to make a below the line response, I take a moment to consider what might things look like from their perspective? Why might they be thinking or feeling like this? I then engage and respond with compassion and say something like, 'Oh, that must be tough'. Or I choose not to respond, because if I don't have anything kind to say, it's best not to add to the toxic environment. In doing so, I am kind. Selfishly, when I do this, I find that I am far better as a human than when I called that bloke a goose.

I've always found it helpful to remember that we can't change other people – we can only change ourselves and our reaction to others.

I've always found it helpful to remember that we can't change other people – we can only change ourselves and our reaction to others. I love this because it puts the ball firmly back in our court. What if someone wasn't deliberately trying to annoy you but was instead just doing their best?

What would be different if you were above the line in cultivating compassion and kindness towards others more often? How would your behaviour change? How would your relationships change? How would workplaces be different? How would our world change if we all did this?

What did Sarah do?

Sarah didn't try to rush things or push any feelings down or away. She sat with them. She processed what had happened to her. She didn't beat herself up. Instead, she allowed herself to feel all the feelings. She was whole-hearted and gave her wounds time to heal. She rested and recovered and was gentle with herself. She didn't say, 'I shouldn't be feeling like this', or, 'I should be over this by now'. She validated her own experience without allowing it to shame her.

Sarah was compassionate towards herself and ended up embracing the opportunity to grow. She also focussed on being the best leader she could be for her team and giving them support.

Reflection questions

What resonated with you in this chapter?

What insights do you have?

What could you cultivate (grow more of)?

What could you eliminate (do less of)?

If you did this, how would your life be different?

If you did this, who else would benefit?

How would they benefit?

If you don't make a change, what are the consequences?

'The universe is not outside of you. Look inside yourself; everything that you want, you already are.'

Rumi

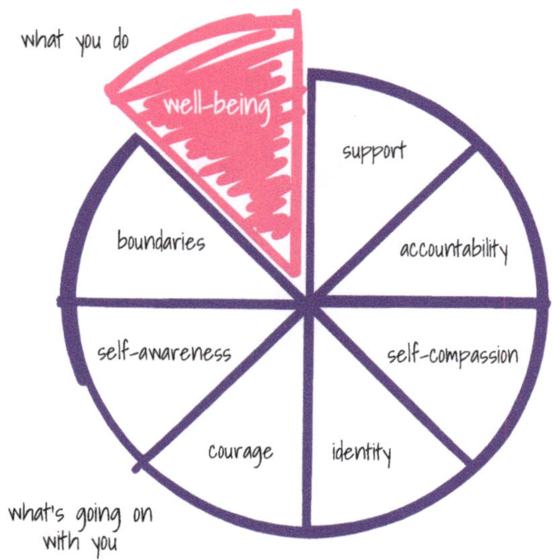

Figure 23: A self-cultivated leader prioritises well-being

Putting the work into your well-being

Do you remember the song that says, 'You don't know what you've got until it's gone'? In late 2016, I totally lost my well-being, and ever since, I've been experimenting and discovering how to get it back.

My mother, Anne, had been ill with ovarian cancer for four and a half years, and she died in mid-2016. She was the absolute glue of our family and such a special person to all who knew her. It's been a huge loss for us all. Throughout her illness and after her death, I was navigating the great unknown of grief. What do you do? How do you grieve? I didn't know how and I hadn't been looking after myself at all, with weight gain, no exercise and becoming a bit of a social hermit.

After Mum's death, I was hit out of nowhere by the truck of peri-menopause. I'd never heard of it – that time before menopause where you get all the symptoms but still have intermittent periods. Bang! Anxiety, panic attacks, sleeplessness, hot flushes, cramping, severe fatigue, anger and on and on. One article I came across listed thirty-seven symptoms of peri-menopause.

So I decided to take control, make some changes and prioritise my well-being. It's been up and down and challenging, but I've learnt that well-being is like a muscle. You just need to keep flexing. It's like exercise, and you need to do it consistently. You can't just go on a holiday for two weeks once a year while neglecting yourself the rest of the time and thinking that will fix you. It's like going to a gym session and thinking that will be enough to set you up to run a marathon.

But I'm no lone ranger in not looking after my well-being. For some reason, many of us find it easier to look after everyone else but neglect ourselves – we don't take the time for self-cultivation, and some of us don't even know what that means or how to do it.

We say we're too busy, we don't have time, we'll go for that run tomorrow, we'll just do a scroll through social media before going to bed. Before we know it, we're burnt out – forced to stop and take time off work to rest and recover. It can take a long time to patch ourselves up.

I can't tell you how many stories I've heard of where someone has been too busy to take time off and has worked unsustainable hours until they crash and need to take six months off to heal.

Know what nourishes you

Reflecting on the consequences of not looking after my well-being and listening to many people (particularly women) in my network who experienced similar issues, I realised that well-being and self-care are foundational leadership skills. I wanted to introduce them into my leadership and team programs so that more people could gain the support and skills they needed to make positive interventions before getting to burn out and suffering mental health issues.

Leading yourself first and being a self-cultivated person means nurturing and nourishing your well-being. What does it mean to you? Do you know what gives you energy? Do you know what fills your cup up? Do you know what depletes you and drains your battery? Well-being is an entirely individual thing.

A group of women attended one of my Well-being Workshops for Busy Women. When asked to explain what well-being meant to them, they responded with a variety of mental, physical and spiritual factors:

- Quiet time
- Relationship with an intimate partner
- Spirituality
- Creativity
- Possibilities
- New day/start afresh
- Social connection
- Peace/calm
- Challenge
- Goals
- Mentally uplifting
- Being present
- Walking in nature.

Gallup defined well-being as the difference between a thriving life and a struggling or suffering life. There are five essential elements for thriving, and we can do something about each of them:

Career well-being: You like what you do every day

Social well-being: You have meaningful friendships in your life

Financial well-being: You manage your money well

Physical well-being: You have the energy to get things done

Community well-being: You like where you live.

Gallup described career well-being as the most important element. It is the foundation for the other four because work plays such a big part in most people's lives (Gallup, 2021).

Getting off the treadmill

Many of us are constantly running on a treadmill in this high-performance world of more, more, more. All we can think about is surviving and getting through each day. Constantly busy, we are like hamsters on a wheel, going around and around every day – but where are we going? How do we keep up the pace?

The answer is that we can't.

Rather than feeling frustrated by our limitations, we must figure out our strengths and build on those. Gallup suggests that if we use our top five strengths every day, we are six times more likely to be engaged in work and three times more likely satisfied with our own lives. If we use these strengths each day, we are thirty-eight per cent more likely to be productive, forty-four per cent more likely to give customer satisfaction and fifty per cent more likely to have

Rather than feeling frustrated by our limitations, we must figure out our strengths and build on those.

high retention (Flade, Asplund, & Elliot, 2015). To understand your strengths, a tool like the VIA Survey on Character Strengths (VIA Institute on Character, 2021) is a great start.

I developed the following model to help clients evaluate their well-being. It looked at how important using our strengths and having self-awareness are to our well-being.

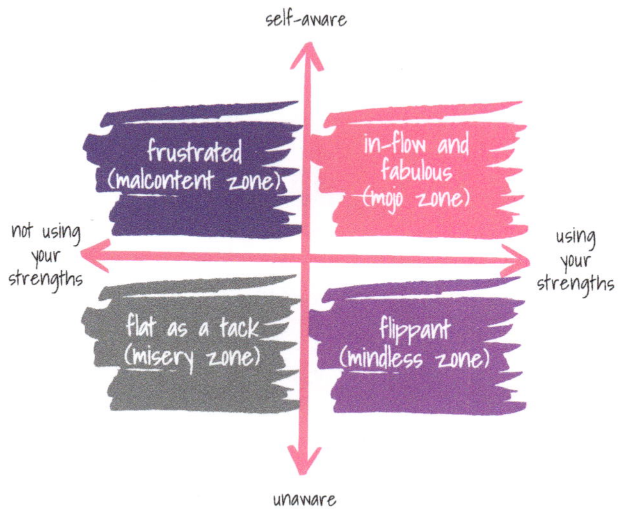

Figure 24: How strengths and self-awareness boost your mojo

Feeling in-flow and fabulous. This is the Mojo Zone! You're able to be you. You're aware of your top strengths and what you're like at your best, and apply your strengths daily at work and home. You feel engaged, energised and you enjoy what you do.

Positive psychology expert Dr Michelle McQuaid says the secret to using your strengths effectively is to ensure you're choosing the right one, in the right amount and at the right time. This is called the 'golden mean' of our strengths; we're neither underusing nor overusing them. Doing so can also be detrimental to ourselves and others in our life (McQuaid, 2021).

Feeling flat as a tack. This is the Misery Zone. You lack self-awareness about your strengths and what you're like at your best, or you have a blind spot. In addition, you're not regularly using one or more of your key strengths.

It's easy to become stuck when you're in this zone and feel like there's something not quite right or feel low on energy. You're unaware that you need to find ways to understand or reconnect with your strengths and apply them regularly in your life to turn things around. You need to find ways to be more you! There's so much positive growth ahead if you accept the challenge to do the inner work, develop your understanding and get clear about what you're like at your best.

Proactively search for ways to apply your strengths at work and in your personal life. It might be picking up a new hobby at home. Or you might have a conversation with your boss to identify ways you can apply your strengths at work more often with the support of your workplace.

Feeling frustrated. This is the Malcontent Zone. You're self-aware enough to understand the importance of using your strengths, and you know your top strengths, but you're unable to find enough ways to apply them regularly or you're holding them back and dimming your light.

Re-visit your strengths and remember when you were in the Mojo Zone. What were you doing then? What could you learn from what worked in the past and apply to today? What's holding you back from using your strengths?

Feeling Flippant. This is the Mindless Zone. You feel good as you can use your strengths regularly, but you take this for granted and are oblivious about the reason. If something changes and you can't use your strengths, you'll quickly move to the Misery Zone without understanding what's happened or how you can get yourself back to feeling good.

In this zone, you might also be missing out on opportunities to feel even better by using your strengths in the right amount and at the right time. Your opportunity right now is to develop your self-awareness and understand your strengths.

What did Sarah do?

In our coaching sessions, Sarah had the space to realise that she needed to take time off work immediately to rest. Her first step was to take two days off. That doesn't sound long, but even in that brief time, she realised she had been so overwhelmed and consumed by work that she hadn't been present for her family and had lost touch with her usual self. She had lost her joy. She hadn't been true to herself. Sarah identified that she was struggling and not looking after herself and that this was affecting both work and home. She said, 'If I'm not myself at home, then I can't be myself at work and vice versa.'

Sarah put work into her well-being so that it became part of her regular practice. She invested in herself. Over the following months, she became intentional about her values and what was important to her. She paid attention and noticed where she thrived and where she felt stymied. She identified what she could control to improve her well-being and took action. Small steps like switching off devices after a particular time, doing reflection and planning on a Friday to set herself up for the next week, putting a do not disturb notification on her phone and feeding her chooks with a cup of tea in her hand.

Reflection questions

What resonated with you in this chapter?

What insights do you have?

What could you cultivate (grow more of)?

What could you eliminate (do less of)?

If you did this, how would your life be different?

If you did this, who else would benefit?

How would they benefit?

If you don't make a change, what are the consequences?

16
Cultivating Accountability

'Once you learn how to call yourself out on your own bullshit, you can start using it as a fertiliser for growth.'

Stacie Martin

(Martin, 2021)

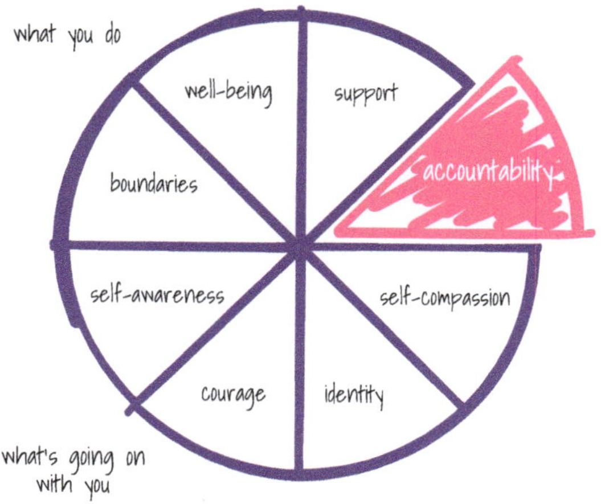

Figure 25: A self-cultivated leader is accountable

Start accountability with yourself

I was working with a team whose self-awareness had been increasing. We were building skills like having difficult conversations and talking about behaviours the team would like to see more or less of. At the end of the program, we went around the room, and each team member shared a behaviour they would like to work on and the action they would take. One of the more vocal and dominant group members had cracked plenty of jokes during the day, but in the final round, Craig was uncharacteristically quiet and spoke last.

He took a deep breath and said, 'I wasn't going to share this, but I've decided I will. I've realised that, at times, I have taken pleasure in other people in the team failing. They've come to me for advice, and I've been judgemental and impatient. I want to show leadership and be better than that. I need to make some changes as that's not the person I want to be, and it's not appropriate for the level I'm at or the role I'm in. I want to step up, listen more and help the team.'

You could have heard a pin drop. Everyone was blown away by Craig's vulnerability, openness and honesty. It was one of the most powerful, personal accountability commitments I'd ever witnessed in a group.

This was someone who had deeply reflected and dared to recognise, name and own an uncomfortable truth about himself. He'd uncovered a blind spot. He also recognised that this was a great growth opportunity. By sharing his learning, he let his team know that he was committed to change and invited them to support him to do so.

The personal accountability model (figure 19) shows how important trust and self-awareness are in holding ourselves accountable and uncovering our blind spots, especially in front of others.

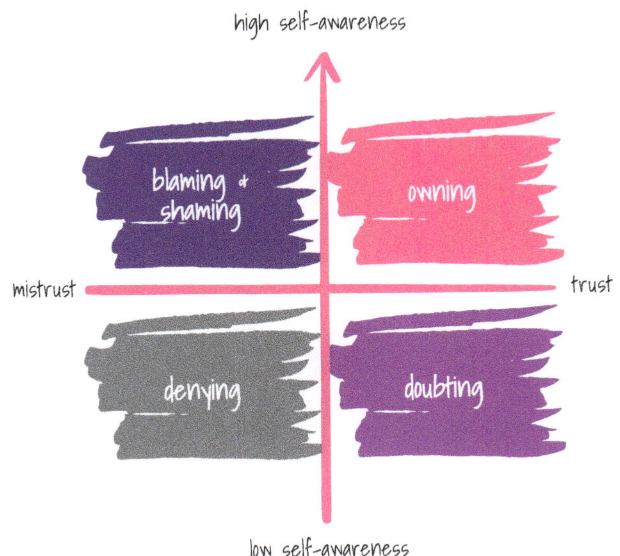

Figure 26: A model for personal accountability

There are four stages in taking responsibility for ourselves, and change involves growth in self-awareness and building trust.

Owning

Through the learning we'd done together, Craig's self-awareness had increased, and he was in an environment of trust with his team. That meant he could take ownership of his behaviour and ask his team for support. This had the flow-on effect of building trust within the team as asking for help showed vulnerability. No one shot him down, and he was accepted, further increasing the team's psychological safety.

A self-cultivated person recognises and owns their blind spots. They realise that this is an empowering process that can transform our behaviour and relationships. Ownership requires a high trust environment to listen and have conversations with others and high self-awareness to reconcile the external feedback with your internal sense of self and to respond and make positive change.

Doubting

You can hear what others are saying in a high trust environment because you feel safe and aren't in threat or defensive mode. If your self-awareness is low, you're not sure what to do with the feedback or how to use it to change your behaviour. That means you spend a lot of time doubting and second-guessing yourself, and can't take personal accountability for change.

Denying

A low trust environment with high self-awareness can lead us to deny our blind spots and not take accountability. Because we are acting out of the amygdala, we lack perspective on our behaviour and its impact. In a high trust environment, we would recognise our behaviour and take responsibility, but when there's low trust, our judgement and performance are impeded, and we can't think clearly.

Blaming and shaming

A low trust environment destroys empathy. We lose any ability to connect with others and stand in their shoes. Our mirror neurons deactivate, and we feel threatened and move into protective behaviours. If we also have low self-awareness, this combination can lead to blaming and shaming behaviour – it's not us, it's them! They are wrong, and we are right.

Or we might be self-aware, but mistrust causes our lens on the world to narrow. We're afraid that if we show weakness or admit fault, we won't be accepted and will somehow be punished. We see a lot of this behaviour from leaders in government and some industry leaders.

What did Sarah do?

Sarah is one of the most accountable people I've had the pleasure of coaching. She faces her demons, asks herself difficult questions, uncovers her blind spots and looks fully at herself in the mirror. She took this major setback as an opportunity for growth and development.

At the end of each coaching session, she wrote down her goals and actions. She read the notes I sent her from our sessions and reflected upon them before the next. She ticked off the actions she set herself and reported on them. By participating in the coaching process, she set up a system and gave herself the necessary space and structure to be accountable to herself.

That she could be professional, give her best to her team and the organisation despite personal disappointment and then move to a new organisation was all down to her hard work. There was no luck involved, and it didn't just happen. She created it by following through and doing the hard, deep and brave work of self-development.

Reflection questions

What resonated with you in this chapter?

What insights do you have?

What could you cultivate (grow more of)?

What could you eliminate (do less of)?

If you did this, how would your life be different?

If you did this, who else would benefit?

How would they benefit?

If you don't make a change, what are the consequences?

17

Cultivating Identity

'When we feel at home within ourselves, we can enjoy life and each other, just as we are. We can nurture honest, uplifting connections with others in which our sense of integrity and self-esteem flourish. Together we can share our inspiration and motivation for life, encouraging each other to see that when we feel at home within ourselves, we may feel at home in our bonds with each other and the world around us too. Indeed, when at home within, we are home wherever we are.'

Meredith Gaston

(Gaston, 2017)

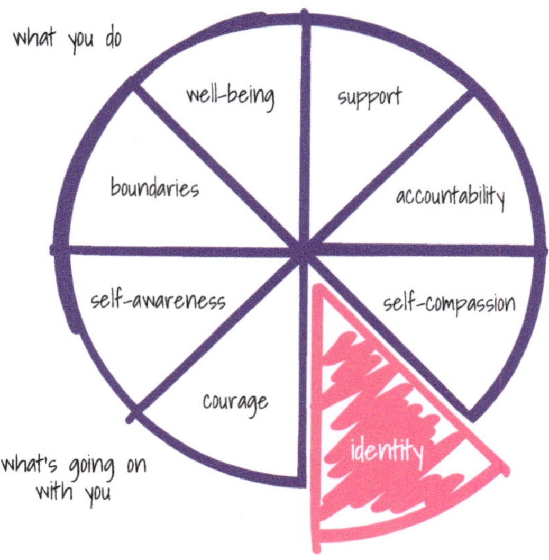

Figure 27: A self-cultivated leader regularly upgrades their identity

Upgrade your self-image

When did you last spring clean your wardrobe? It means going through all the clothes and examining them in the light of day. You throw out clothes that don't fit anymore. You might discard clothes from a time when you had a particular persona. Perhaps it was that goth phase that you went through at uni. You realise those clothes don't reflect who you are now, so you decide to get rid of them.

You might discover some clothes tucked away at the back of the cupboard that you'd forgotten about and realise that you still really love them. Once you've thrown out a whole heap of stuff and made space in your wardrobe, you might look around and decide you need to buy new clothes that reflect who you are now. They say we should dress for the job that we want, not the job that we have. So it's time to buy clothes that reflect the person you want to be in the future.

We spring clean our wardrobes, our offices, our gardens, and our homes. But when did you last spring clean your identity or self-image? Both work in a similar way to our wardrobes.

We all have stories and beliefs about ourselves – who we are and what we're capable of. But how often do we stop to pause, shine a light and examine who we think we are? When do we ensure that our beliefs about ourselves truly reflect who we are now and who we want to be in the future?

When do we ensure that our beliefs about ourselves truly reflect who we are now and who we want to be in the future?

We develop beliefs about ourselves that stem from when we were children or from difficult times as a teenager. Or from a bad experience at work. Some of these self-beliefs are not useful, and we need to get rid of them.

The number one priority for most of my coaching clients who step into leadership roles has been identifying who they are as leaders – what they stand for and who they want to be known as. They've determined that their lack of clarity around their leadership identity is a barrier to stepping into their power. They've realised it's time to upgrade their personal story about who they are as a leader to improve their performance and remove roadblocks to their success.

If we don't regularly examine and upgrade our beliefs about ourselves, it's like using an old paper roadmap to navigate life and make decisions instead of upgrading to a GPS that constantly updates and reflects what's current in the world. Imagine you want to drive somewhere you've never been before, and your old paper map can't tell you how to get there because new roads have been built. What happens? You know where you want to go, but your system won't tell you how to get there.

It's the same with our personal identity. We may have taken on a new role and identified some goals we aspire to, but if old beliefs about what we're capable of are floating around in our subconscious, chances are we'll end up sabotaging ourselves because we haven't upgraded our old map of the world. We bump up against beliefs about what we're capable of, which get in the way of achieving our goals.

Start from the inside out

James Clear is the author of the best-selling book ***Atomic Habits***. In explaining why this practice is so integral to our success as leaders, he says there are three levels of change: a change in outcomes, a change in processes, or a change in identity (Clear, 2018).

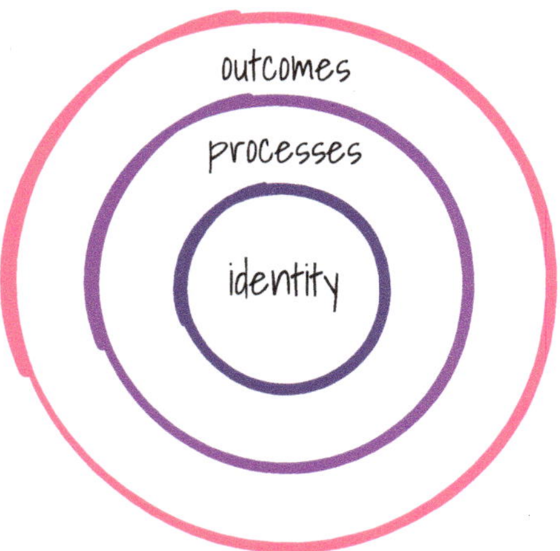

Figure 28: Change in identity, processes and outcomes. (James Clear)

Many successful and unsuccessful people have goals they want to achieve, but why do only some people achieve them? James Clear believes that many of us work from the outside circle inwards when wanting to change. He believes that starting from the inside, from our identity, would be more effective. Instead of focusing on outcomes (or **what** we want to achieve), he recommends we try focusing on **who** we wish to become and build identity-based habits.

A self-cultivated person regularly examines their beliefs about themselves. They can recognise which no longer serve them and replace them with more helpful beliefs.

What did Sarah do?

During our coaching sessions, we explored Sarah's leadership identity. She had never done this before, but she wanted to own her role and what she brought to it – whatever forum she was in. She even identified a motivational mantra to help stay connected.

She discovered that, at some point, she had developed a belief about not speaking up in meetings with senior leadership. She didn't know where it had stemmed from, but she recognised it. When I asked her to visualise it, she said, 'It's like I'm wearing a veil'. The veil was translucent so she could see through it, and it blocked her from being seen by others. She said she was hiding behind it, so senior management didn't see the amazing leader that her team saw every day.

Through coaching, Sarah shone a light on the unconscious belief she had around her leadership identity. As she said it aloud, she realised she'd been letting it dictate her behaviour. She'd been on autopilot, so when she made the unconscious conscious, she started doing things differently.

During our session, she said, 'I can control my thoughts about this change process. I can recognise the negative talk, the perceptions I hold and shift them to a better mindset and more useful beliefs.'

Sarah determined to tell her story in the right language to the people in her organisation who needed to hear it. She would speak more about what she was doing during her one-on-one catchups with her director. She was intentional about how she behaved in meetings. She prepared well to set herself up for success and be in the right mindset to lead. Sarah took control, played her role as leader, brought people together and set the expectations. She was able to step into her personal power and lift the veil.

Reflection questions

What resonated with you in this chapter?

What insights do you have?

What could you cultivate (grow more of)?

What could you eliminate (do less of)?

If you did this, how would your life be different?

If you did this, who else would benefit?

How would they benefit?

If you don't make a change, what are the consequences?

PART THREE

A Cultivating Leader

'It's more important to be a good person than it is to be a good tennis player. Being a good human is absolutely my priority every single day.'

Ash Barty

(Chowdhury, 2021)

Create an environment where your people can thrive

One team manager I worked with described the stark difference between working with a cultivating leader and one who operates below the line.

'When Tom joined our organisation as unit manager, there was an instant lack of trust. He was excellent technically, could talk the talk and had a PhD, but it soon became apparent he was not a people manager. He didn't trust us, his senior managers, or his people and thought people were out to get him. He was an extreme micro-manager, needing to know every detail and oversee everything. He even told me that I should let him know every time one of my staff left the state – even though it was my job to decide this. When I pushed back, his response was, "I don't care about your authorisation. You will tell me when your staff leave this state."

'We protected our staff a lot. They knew what was going on but only saw a half of it. As senior managers, we lived under extreme stress. He would try to bring you down and tell you things other people had supposedly said about you that weren't true. It was just to try to put you back in your box.

'One of my colleagues was looking at further development opportunities and asked for his advice. A leader is supposed to nurture and guide your career. Tom told my colleague that he had no future in our industry, as he lacked technical capability, was useless, and no one respected him. He told staff during a workshop that no one in the industry liked them and that they were the most technically incompetent staff in the state. He then left the room and left us, his managers, to deal with the fallout and try to reassure staff.

'He was threatened by anyone in the team who was respected, knowledgeable and who showed initiative. He yelled at staff, wouldn't share information and was extremely competitive. Meetings were always tense as he destroyed the team and people's confidence.

'He would listen to gossip from external stakeholders and take their criticisms as gospel rather than back the team. When an external stakeholder criticised the technical capability of our staff, his response was to try to introduce a process to make all staff sit a three-hour technical exam (even if they were support staff with no training in the area). He then expected staff to write a technical paper on a topic he proposed and be interviewed by a panel of external stakeholders who could ask anything. This was to staff with university qualifications who had worked with us for twenty years. At the last minute, the process didn't go ahead because of intervention from others.

'The impact was that we had so many staff on stress leave, who lost confidence and who couldn't cope. They were too frightened to do stuff because they might get it wrong and get shot down. He took away their ability to learn and train and wouldn't back their judgement. Eventually, twenty staff left the team, and stakeholders were laughing at us.

'Contrast this with our current leader, Mike, who is the complete opposite. He creates a calm environment where there is trust and respect and a lot more talking and care for staff. He asks, "What do you want to do? How are you coping mentally? What do you need to do for your family situation?"

'He has rebuilt the program by attracting new investment and is great with stakeholders. The environment is so much more productive – we are now with a leader who nurtures our development and fosters our growth. He also has great foresight and knows industry strategy, so we've been able to work in new and exciting areas and have a future. We are now the best technical team, and we are high-performing. But we aren't pushed, and we don't compete against each other. Since Mike has been in charge, it's human-first.'

I'm lucky enough to work with many rural and regional leaders like Mike. A cultivating leader nourishes and nurtures. They also prune and shape and encourage their staff to grow and develop. Some of the things they have in common are:

- They trust their staff
- They are kind and have compassion
- They are vulnerable where appropriate and are human-centred
- They know what is going on in their staff's lives and are connected with them
- They see the potential of their team and want them to succeed
- They are concerned about the mental health and well-being of their staff
- They believe in their staff
- They expect accountability from staff
- They stand up for their staff and try to push back on unrealistic demands from senior management
- They want their team to be excellent
- They want their team to be sustainable
- They are willing to have tough, honest conversations with staff
- They are emotionally courageous

I've identified Six Keys to being a cultivating leader.

In Part Three, we'll use each key to unlock a clear path.

THE FIRST KEY:

A Cultivating Leader Creates Psychological Safety

'One of the criticisms I've faced over the years is that I'm not aggressive enough, or assertive enough, or maybe somehow, because I'm empathetic, it means I'm weak. I totally rebel against that. I refuse to believe that you cannot be both compassionate and strong.'

Jacinda Ardern,
Prime Minister of New Zealand

Make it safe

One of the foundations of a great team is psychological safety – where everyone feels they can be themselves at work and speak up without fear of being judged or punished (Edmondson, 2019). Google research found that people in teams with high psychological safety brought in more revenue, were rated as effective twice as often by executives, were more likely to take on new roles, and stayed with the company (Google, 2021).

I spoke recently with a client who took on a twelve-month secondment to another part of his organisation. Steve is a confident, capable, highly professional, calm and positive person. He's dedicated to being a better leader and has aspirations to become a senior leader in the business. He values process and results. I hadn't spoken to him since he returned from his secondment.

'So how are you, Steve, and how did the secondment go?' I asked.

'Cynthia, I am hurt,' he said. I could hear it in his voice. He sounded different, more tired, a bit defeated, not his usual exuberant self, and he'd lost a bit of his spark.

He explained that the leader he reported to on his secondment was very challenging. 'She was not a people-person,' he said. 'It was all about the task; there was no appreciation. The workload was unrealistic; the ask wasn't fair. She wasn't polite, there was no respect, and she micro-managed me. She would speak over me in meetings with stakeholders. There has to be some genuineness towards people, and she didn't have any.

'For the last twelve months, I haven't thought about leadership at all. I was down, reactive, surviving. I wasn't in a growth mindset. My wife was worried; she could see the toll it was taking on me.

'I was recently offered a job in another area for a significant pay rise, but I said no. It wasn't worth the money. I just wanted to come back to work for my old manager James. I just want to feel safe. I've now seen the other side of managing people, and I will never treat my team like that. Now I know who I don't want to be. James is such a great manager because he cares for his people.'

Being the person of character and the optimist that he is, Steve used the negative experience to reflect on his own leadership and courageously pinpointed some changes he could make to his practice. He identified that he'd been micro-managing his team, and when experiencing this on his secondment, he realised how detrimental to morale and performance it could be. Some of the practices Steve thought were helping keep people accountable, he now realised made his staff feel judged, watched and under pressure.

'I was managing the process so tightly,' he said. 'I've relaxed my grip coming back. This team has accountability, is experienced, and we respect each other. I've let go, and it feels really great. I feel I'm not carrying the weight. The team has relaxed – they are not in alert mode. Before when I spoke to them, they were like, "Oh no, what have I done now?" Now that I've relaxed, I know my team will deliver better because they are free.'

That is what psychological safety means – people are free to be themselves, not coming to work in fear. Steve experienced what it was like to work for a leader with no trust or respect and saw how that impacted him as a human and a team member. The negative effects of not feeling safe bled into his personal life. It was interesting that he used the word 'hurt' to describe the state he was in. He meant wounded, diminished, damaged. He needed to come back to a safe haven to recover and get himself back. That was what James' cultivating leadership provided.

Own your part

Even the greatest leaders can have moments of being human. We all have blind spots and revert to autopilot behaviour. We can feel frustrated, react rather than choose to respond and be below the line without realising it. If leaders do too much of this and create a pattern rather than just moments, the effect on the team can be an unsafe environment. However, if the leader has created a psychologically safe environment and then drops below the line, team members can speak up and call out the behaviour, knowing all will be OK. What a gift to the team! Everyone, no matter what their position, can learn and grow together.

One of the most outstanding leaders I know is an absolute dynamo. She is challenging, inspirational, generous, kind, savvy, strategic, and transformational. She is a good human.

As we worked together in a team, we had many meetings where I felt she spoke to me in a manner that left me feeling diminished, ashamed and not respected. Consequently, I began to second-guess my behaviour, felt anxious, hesitant about speaking up and contributing. I was confused. What should I do?

I decided to talk with her. I felt safe to do so as I knew she had great integrity and was probably unaware of the impact of her behaviour on me. Even though I knew this, I still had to summon my courage and stretch myself to have the conversation. It was uncomfortable, but I knew I had a choice to say it and deal with it or ignore it but carry on feeling resentful and being a victim.

Sure enough, when I raised the issue, she apologised straight away. She was unaware of what she'd done and thanked me for being courageous in raising it, as she understood it would have been difficult to do. Then she encouraged me to step up and claim a greater role in the group and talked about the value I added, how I could contribute more. What started out as a difficult conversation ended up being an extremely positive interaction. This leader modelled for me how to receive feedback gracefully and effectively.

As a result, we continued working together well, and the trust between us grew. I felt safe to be myself, so I stepped up more in the group and grew confident as I challenged myself to exercise my courage muscle. The whole team benefitted because my voice was heard.

But imagine if the leader hadn't made it safe for me to provide feedback? Imagine if she'd been defensive, invalidated me, hadn't listened, shamed or blamed me, or told me to stop being so sensitive? That would have eroded psychological safety and trust and meant that the team would have been negatively affected. I may have disengaged and stopped contributing, and my voice would have disappeared. I would have dreaded each meeting and lost further confidence. What's more, I would never have provided feedback to that leader again.

The research agrees

Carol Dweck is a psychologist, author and pioneering researcher in motivation, why people succeed (or don't), and how to foster success. She says that in a growth mindset, challenges are exciting rather than threatening. So rather than thinking, 'Oh, I'm going to reveal my weaknesses,' you say, 'Wow, here's a chance to grow' (Dweck, 2007).

Psychologically safe team members feel confident that no one will be embarrassed or punished for admitting a mistake, asking a question, or offering a new idea. From a neuroscience perspective, we become more open-minded, resilient, motivated, solution-finding, creative and persistent when we feel safe. We

> From a neuroscience perspective, we become more open-minded, resilient, motivated, solution-finding, creative and persistent when we feel safe.

perform better and connect with others more effectively. Conversely, when we're under threat and don't feel safe, this shuts down perspective and our analytical reasoning. Our brains cannot perform at their best.

One of my clients told me of a team member who had reached out to their leader for help, only to be told, 'I can't believe you're asking me that. You should know how to do that!'

The team member felt ashamed and decided the leader didn't care about them. Trust was destroyed; he does not feel safe with the leader and will never ask for his help again. What a lost opportunity. Imagine the difference had the leader expressed care, thanked the person for the question, and coached them to find a solution? The rest of the team knows what has happened, which doesn't help the leader build trust.

Dr Michelle McQuaid found that if a manager expresses care, compassion and appreciation, it positively impacts our sense of thriving at work, affecting job performance, job satisfaction, and workplace commitment. Although the research found that expressing care for workers benefits the manager's well-being more than the team, it's a win-win situation (The Well-Being Lab, 2021).

We will dig more into the concept of psychological safety later in Part Four: A Cultivating Culture.

Reflection questions

What resonated with you in this chapter?

What insights do you have about your leadership?

What could you cultivate (grow more of)?

What could you eliminate (do less of)?

If you did this, how would your life be different?

If you did this, who else would benefit?

How would they benefit?

If you don't make a change, what are the consequences?

19

THE SECOND KEY:
A Cultivating Leader Creates Leaders

'Old Rule: Lead with dominance. Create followers. New Rule: Lead with humility. Cultivate leaders.'

Abby Wambach

(Wambach, 2019)

Build others

One behaviour my survey people admired most, was leaders helping others to grow and develop. They valued leaders who provided support and encouragement for all staff to move forward. Leaders who were mentors built people up and genuinely wanted others to do well. Leaders who were willing to share, opened doors and offered a hand up in careers and professions. Leaders who brought others along with them and who valued diversity.

Does this describe the leaders in your organisation, industry or community?

A producer I spoke with is on several agri-food and industry boards. She says their industry shuts people out, and she puts it down to those in power who want to retain their power. She has seen people try to make positive change and then experience bullying and take a step back. They are 'thrown under the bus'. Many leaders have been demonstrating poor behaviour for decades. 'It's a cultural problem in our industry, and we need to start calling it out, it's not acceptable.'

As an industry leader, she says part of her remit is finding new talent – doing as much as she can and then stepping back. But she has noticed the same leaders recycled around different organisations across the industry. 'It's no surprise that the chairs have been the same for forty years.' She's seen people blocking others from having the knowledge they've got. 'They have so much power but haven't allowed other people to flourish. There are a lot of big egos, and you hear them say, "There's no-one else that will do it." But real leaders look to replace themselves.

'We need to tap people on the shoulder to get involved. We need to diversify our networks to recruit far more broadly than we've done in the past. As leaders, we need to be forever thinking about our succession plan. We need a supply chain of leaders at different levels.'

Position future leaders

This perspective of industry leadership is backed up by a discussion I had with emerging leaders a few years ago. A comment from one participant still sticks clearly in my mind. Cameron said, 'We're dying to get involved in our industry, but when we walk up to the doors, they get closed in our faces.'

It was such a powerful metaphor for his experience of attempting involvement in leadership roles in his industry. And he wasn't the only one; other people in the program shared similar experiences.

Yet it conflicted with what I was hearing from people already in leadership positions, who said, 'We'd love to hand onto the next generation, but we can't find anyone.'

How do you ensure you're not closing the door on your emerging leaders if you are a current leader? Often it's easiest to go with our existing network and with people that we already know. We have a bias to select people like ourselves – that's the path of least resistance. But proactive recruitment of a broad array of leaders at different levels requires more work.

If you want to ensure your team, organisation, industry, or community is vibrant, relevant and future-focused, you need to make sure that all the voices are heard and included. The path of least resistance in recruitment for leadership just doesn't cut it anymore.

You need to understand the different voices in your industry or organisation. Who is not sitting at the table? Who is missing? Where do they hang out? As a leader, how can you strategically

> If you want to ensure your team, organisation, industry, or community is vibrant, relevant and future-focused, you need to make sure that all the voices are heard and included.

and proactively connect with them to understand their perspectives and needs? How can you help them better navigate and understand their industry? What advice can you give them around the skills they need and how to position themselves to have a positive profile?

If you do this, you will ensure your industry or organisation is strongly positioned for the future.

Cultivating leaders value diversity. They recognise it as strength and aren't afraid of it. As Audre Lorde explained, 'In our work and in our living, we must recognise that difference is a reason for celebration and growth, rather than a reason for destruction' (Hall, 2004).

Lead by example

Cathy McGowan is one leader with a remarkable ability to cultivate other leaders. She is the past president of Australian Women in Agriculture. As a farmer and rural consultant, she is best known for being elected the independent member for the federal seat of Indi in northeast Victoria in 2013. In doing so, Cathy became the first female independent to sit on the crossbenches.

One of the many things Cathy did to nurture, encourage and inspire more leaders was to run a program of volunteers from her electorate to work in her Canberra office. This program aimed to build the political capability of the community. They would come to Canberra in small groups and play different roles like speech writing, administration tasks, representing Cathy at meetings and attending political functions. They gained insight into how politics was done at the federal level. I was fortunate enough to be on this program as I had grown up in the Indi electorate.

Every morning, Cathy would sit with the volunteers and hold a comprehensive briefing about tasks. At the end of each day, she would debrief and ask each person to reflect on what they had learnt. I was astounded at her generosity, calm, care and stamina. No matter what was going on in this pressure-cooker environment, she listened and ensured that the volunteers learned from their experience. She wanted them to take back what they had learnt to their workplaces and community and have more confidence and capacity to engage in the political process.

After leaving federal politics, Cathy, along with other committed people, held a national convention to build the capacity of people to run as independents. It had never been done before, but she set a bold vision and got others on board. Cathy and her network brought people together to build confidence and networks, and share ideas and inspiration about running for office. Since then, Cathy and two other inspiring women from northeast Victoria, Jill Briggs and Alana Johnson, have been working to cultivate other leaders across Australia at different levels of politics to take charge of their futures and run as independents. Cathy is about power with, not power over.

One of the many things I respect about her (even if it is sometimes annoying!) is that she refuses to have anyone put their monkey on her back. If you go to her with a problem, she always puts it back on you to solve it by asking, 'So what are you going to do about it?' This leader cultivates others by encouraging and challenging them to come up with their own solutions.

Imagine what our rural communities, industries and organisations would be like with more leaders cultivating and nurturing other leaders. There is so much power in that. What if we welcomed people into the tent and at the table with the attitude that everyone is a leader and has something valuable to offer.

Reflection questions

What resonated with you in this chapter?

What insights do you have about your leadership?

What could you cultivate (grow more of)?

What could you eliminate (do less of)?

If you did this, how would your life be different?

If you did this, who else would benefit?

How would they benefit?

If you don't make a change, what are the consequences?

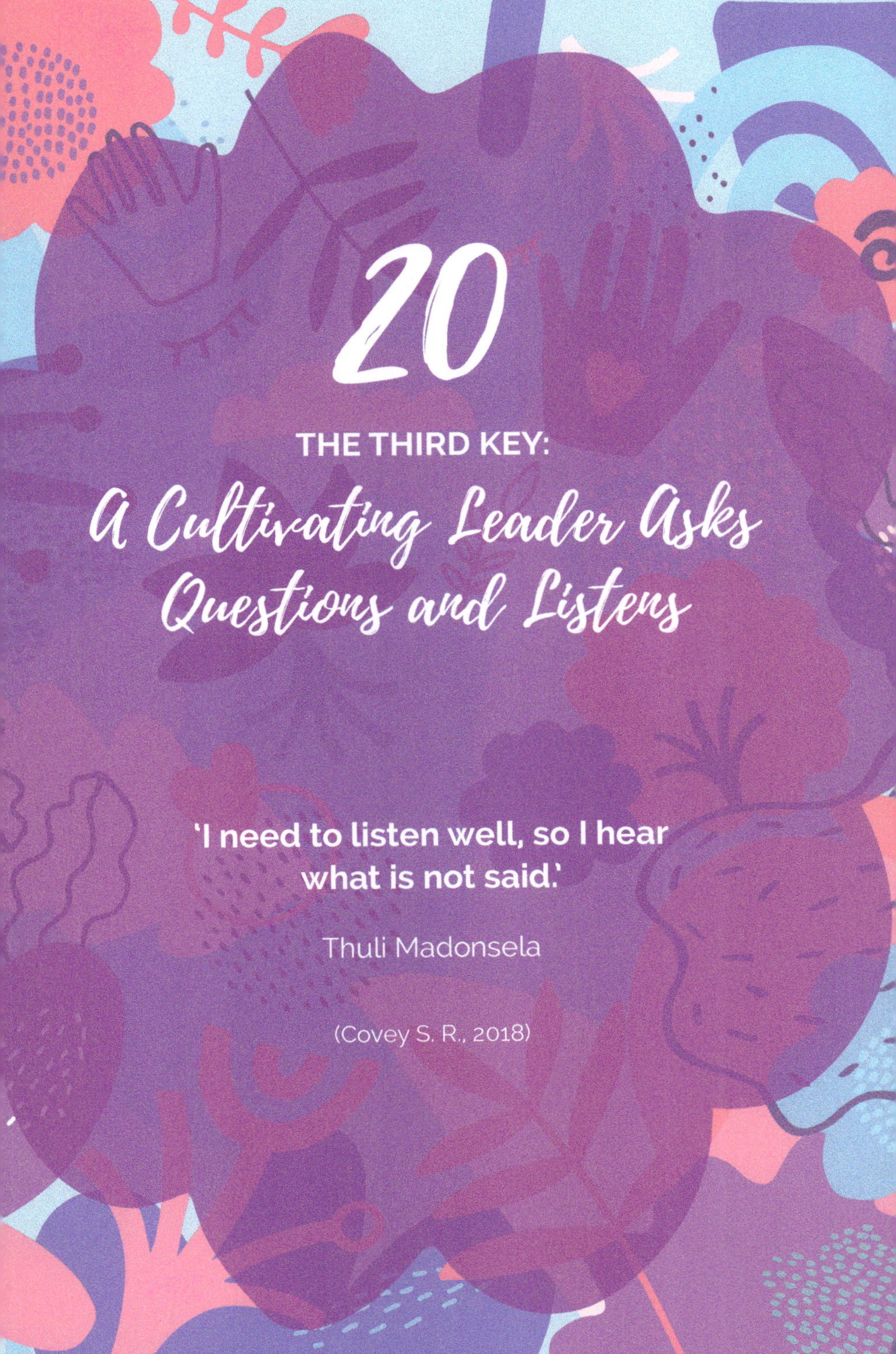

20

THE THIRD KEY:
A Cultivating Leader Asks Questions and Listens

'I need to listen well, so I hear what is not said.'

Thuli Madonsela

(Covey S. R., 2018)

Seek first to understand

Thomas was a participant in an emerging leaders program I was facilitating. On Day One, he expressed frustration about a new employee he was managing. He'd observed certain behaviour from this person and leapt to the conclusion that she was 'hopeless and has a bad attitude. I'll tell her to do something, and she just doesn't seem to understand and takes a long time to do things. I'm going to get rid of her.'

Luckily, participating in the leadership program meant he gained new knowledge about different communication styles. He left Day One with strategies that enabled him to check his assumptions and consider other possible explanations for her behaviour. His main conclusion was that perhaps she communicated differently to him and that an alternative style might connect with her more effectively.

So he committed to experimenting with a different way of communicating. The following week, at Day Two, he reported back, saying, 'I changed the way I spoke to her about work that needs doing. I've asked more questions rather than giving her orders, and I've discovered that she is actually really great. She's surprised me with what she's capable of.'

> Our brains don't like not knowing, so we constantly make up stories to fill gaps.

The success of this approach meant his staff member could deliver and be more engaged, productive and happy. His perception of her shifted from being a problem to having skills and value. It was an excellent result for him as a manager, his staff member, and the business.

Our brains don't like not knowing, so we constantly make up stories to fill gaps. It happens in our subconscious, without us being aware of it. We jump to conclusions all the time. We see behaviour and assume we know what it means. However, we can't see another person's motivation for their behaviour, so we often get it wrong.

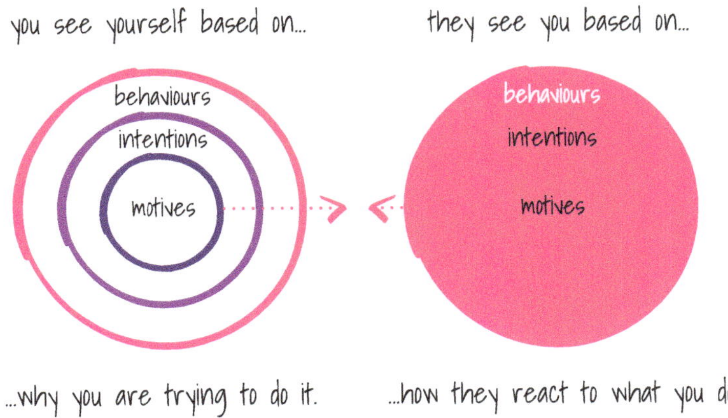

Figure 29: How our motives can be easily misinterpreted by others (Total SDI, 2018)

Thomas saw his staff member struggling to implement instructions and assumed she was hopeless and had a bad attitude. The real problem was that he was delivering information in a way that she couldn't connect with.

A cultivating leader takes the time to discover what is going on for someone, rather than leaping to incorrect conclusions and taking action based on the wrong data. Asking questions is a way of adding new data to our decision-making and checking our assumptions before racing to action.

If Thomas had acted before first seeking to understand, he would have sacked an employee who was actually very good. That is a cost to the business, aside from the personal toll on the employee and her family.

Slow down and listen

Many of us have a bias towards taking action – we just want to get stuff done. Often we do it because we think we don't have time for conversations, but in the end, it's a false economy. Getting stuff done is a strength, but it costs us if it is overdone and we're not taking the time to gather all the data. We don't always know how to have the conversation or even realise we are not considering all the data. Human data is just as necessary as factual data.

A cultivating leader adds listening to their skillset by being curious and understanding what is happening in another person's world. True, deep listening is not easy, yet it is a gift to be seen and heard. Think of the last time someone listened to you. They didn't interrupt to tell you what they thought or talk about their experience. They didn't fidget or look impatient. They didn't try to hurry you along. They didn't invalidate you by telling you not to worry. They just sat and held the space for you to say what you needed to say.

I have a close friend called Nick. Sometimes, despite my best intentions, things go wrong in our conversations. I can tell he doesn't trust my motivations, and this can result in friction and conflict.

Nick expressed a belief that he had a very poor memory that had a debilitating effect on his life. I'd heard him say this before but always tried to respond by encouraging him and saying, 'I don't think it's as bad as you think, I haven't noticed it'. I cared and was worried and wanted to reassure him so that he didn't lose confidence. From my perspective, it didn't seem to be a big issue.

I'd been studying Judith Glaser's work on trust (Glaser J. E., 2014) and the positive effect on our brains of asking questions to understand. I'd also read an article from master coach Marshall

Goldsmith about listening. He says that if someone says they feel you haven't listened, then the proper response is to say, 'I'm sorry. There is no excuse. Please repeat what you just said, and I will try to do better.' (Goldsmith, 2017).

When Nick spoke of his concerns about his memory, I started my usual response and noticed that he was getting agitated. His body language indicated he might get up from the table and leave. He said, 'I've been saying this for years, and no one ever believes me.' I realised that my usual response, although well-intentioned, was invalidating his experience. I was falling into negative behaviours of Knowing ('I know how you feel' – even though I didn't), Limiting (saying there was nothing to worry about, shut down the conversation and invalidating him) and Judging ('I've judged that you have nothing to worry about and I'm judging you for needing to talk about it because everything is OK'). This created mistrust and shut down the conversation.

When I realised what was happening, I immediately changed my response to, 'I am so sorry. I am so sorry that I haven't believed you. Please tell me what it's like for you. I'm listening'. I used positive behaviours of Discovering (asking questions), Expanding (let's continue the conversation) and Appreciating (I appreciate you and want to hear from you).

Nick's body language changed straight away. He re-engaged in the conversation, and his agitation and annoyance disappeared. He opened up about his fears and the impact of the situation on his life. The conversation expanded and went to a whole new level.

It gave me greater insight into myself and my behaviour. I saw how it could come across to others even when unintended and how this affects the quality of relationships. Not truly listening to others destroys trust and sets up a defensive, threat response in another person's brain.

It's a work in progress, and I'm continually practising and learning and making mistakes! Self-compassion is also essential for me in this work – I'm human, with good intentions, and sometimes I get it totally wrong! What about you?

Not truly listening to others destroys trust and sets up a defensive, threat response in another person's brain.

Brené Brown says that 'Leaders must either invest a reasonable amount of time attending to fears and feelings or squander an unreasonable amount of time trying to manage ineffective and unproductive behaviour. If you say, "I do not do fear or feelings," you are not a leader' (Brown B. , 2018).

Listening and asking questions is the primary way for a cultivating leader to deal with fears or feelings.

How often are we too busy to listen? How often do we not take the time to understand another person's perspective? How often do we invalidate others without knowing it?

Reflection questions

What resonated with you in this chapter?

What insights do you have about your leadership?

What could you cultivate (grow more of)?

What could you eliminate (do less of)?

If you did this, how would your life be different?

If you did this, who else would benefit?

How would they benefit?

If you don't make a change, what are the consequences?

21

THE FOURTH KEY:
A Cultivating Leader Practices Emotional Courage

'The key word is practice. Mary Daly, a theologian, writes, "Courage is like – it's a habitus, a habit, a virtue: You get it by courageous acts. It's like you learn to swim by swimming. You learn courage by couraging."'

Brené Brown

(Brown B, 2010)

Leading by example

Simon is a great example of how to be a cultivating leader. His leadership team spoke of the emotional courage and vulnerability he displayed in an all-staff team meeting where they were discussing how staff were feeling about returning to the office after the easing of COVID restrictions. Simon shared that he was feeling very anxious about potentially not working from home as much as he had been.

He recounted that the lockdown and working from home had been ideal for his family dynamic. Simon has a child with special needs, and working from home had been a positive change that provided extra stability and routine for the family and his child. He shed tears as he spoke about his concerns that returning to the office might have on the welfare of his child and the rest of his family. With these worries, he was having trouble sleeping and was experiencing stress and anxiety. Simon said it was important that he and the leadership team understood how all the team members felt and that their well-being was paramount.

His leadership team said how powerful it was that Simon had shared his fears and struggles with the whole team. It signalled to everyone that not being OK was acceptable and made it possible to talk about things. Trust and connection grew with greater psychological safety opening up helpful conversations about concerns. It made known what was previously unknown and allowed them to talk about strategies to support each other and how they might co-create some flexible return to the office policies that worked for the team.

Simon's leadership team were in awe of the positive and courageous leadership he had shown in front of the team and spoke about their respect for him as a leader. They viewed his openness as strength and wanted to help him in whatever way possible. Being real and human and a leader who deeply cares, instead of putting on a façade of having it all together, was precisely the type of leadership that Simon's team needed. There's no reason to pretend you know all the answers and that you are in complete control (high-performing) in these challenging times. Being a cultivating leader served the team.

Show emotional courage

Peter Bregman is the author of *Leading with Emotional Courage.* He says that a lack of emotional courage derails leaders from acting powerfully in their lives, relationships, and work. We avoid following through on uncomfortable actions because we are afraid of feeling the hard feelings. We are unable to sit in discomfort, so we try to move away and shut it down. In other words, it's easier to stay on autopilot because sometimes pressing pause and self-disrupting can be uncomfortable.

Bregman's work shows that increasing your willingness to feel increases your courage to act. When we possess emotional courage, feel discomfort and act anyway, we can have the hard conversations, create accountability and inspire action. He says, 'Any gap you have in emotional courage limits your freedom to act. When you avoid feeling, it's a huge drain on your productivity and your organisational outcomes' (Bregman, 2018).

I've heard the following comments from clients and friends over the past year:

'I'm spending all my time managing this woman's poor behaviour. Everyone else in the community does too, it's exhausting, we're all tiptoeing around her.'

'This person isn't doing their job right, so a few of us have decided we're going to get rid of him.'

'Something's wrong between my friend and me. We went away together for a weekend, and I felt she was quite cold towards me. Even though I've rung her a couple of times, our friendship isn't the same. I don't think I'll bother anymore.'

'One of my team is hopeless, and I'm going to have to move him as he doesn't have the skills to do what I need him to do.'

> To address the fears and feelings of your staff, you need to be willing to sit in discomfort with what these conversations might bring up for you.

Within each of these scenarios, you can see a potential gap in emotional courage. They're avoiding having the initial conversation because they feel uncomfortable. This can escalate conflict and is not helpful behaviour.

To address the fears and feelings of your staff, you need to be willing to sit in discomfort with what these conversations might bring up for you. As well as listening to your staff, emotional courage requires you to take action, not invalidate, minimise or ignore them. Often we do this when we can't have conversations because they make us uncomfortable. If this is you as a leader, then I'd strongly advise you to invest in some coaching to develop your emotional courage muscle.

What does emotional courage look like in a cultivating leader?

- They are calm during a crisis, knowing that emotions are contagious, particularly those of the leader.
- They provide clarity to reduce uncertainty and increase safety.

- They are authentic and honest, even if the message is tough.
- They find ways to support and manage themselves, so they are in a resourceful state.
- They feel discomfort, back themselves and act anyway.
- They initiate and hold difficult conversations with their team, create accountability and inspire action.
- They follow through on tasks, especially the challenging ones.
- They take risks, make decisions and positively influence others.
- They are willing to hear someone's opposing viewpoint, even criticism, without getting defensive.

Face it head-on

In a previous career, I was blindsided by conflict at a team strategic planning workshop. It came from a team member who was acting as team manager. She unleashed a vitriolic tirade saying that she didn't like me and didn't want to work with me. I had no idea that one of my teammates felt so much dislike. Afterwards, on the advice of a mentor, I went to talk to the executive director of our division. He wasn't at the workshop, but I wanted him to know that I was aware of the problem and would do all I could to resolve it.

His response? 'You've got to be kidding me!' he exclaimed incredulously and angrily. 'All of this work we're doing with the team, all of that is because of you! The other women in the team have been coming to me, and I've been working with them, especially the acting team manager, to find a way to deal with you!'

It was one of the most shattering experiences of my working life. After my conversation with the executive director, it emerged that the external facilitator was there to run a workshop with the team to help them deal with me rather than undertake a strategic planning exercise, as I'd been told. It seemed that plenty of work had gone in behind the scenes for quite a while. Many people outside the team, including the executive director and even Human Resources, were involved. Everyone knew what was going on....except for me. No one had spoken to me.

This may sound a bit unbelievable, but it is true. Not one person had ever come to have a conversation with me, and I honestly had no idea what had been going on. It clearly shows how things can escalate when difficult conversations, early on, are avoided. It was a real low point in my career. Twenty years later, I am still deeply affected by the experience and the trauma that was inflicted. However, the experience taught me many valuable lessons about teams, dynamics, below the line behaviour, scapegoating cultures, courage, assumptions, resilience and shame. It also ignited my passion for working with people to build self-awareness. I feel so strongly that we need to do the right thing by others in our teams, behave fairly, and build the skills to have difficult, open conversations about behaviours regularly in our workplaces. If we do, then tricky situations are nipped in the bud, things don't escalate, and people aren't blindsided.

I think that's why Brené Brown's work on courageous leadership resonates so strongly with me. Her mantra is 'Clear is kind. Unclear is unkind' (Brown B. , 2018). We fear being unkind, yet avoiding difficult conversations is more unkind in the long run. It means that we end up talking about others rather than to them. She says of problematic behaviours, 'What this means is that we must find the courage to get curious and possibly surface emotions and emotional experiences that people can't articulate or that might be happening outside their awareness. If we find ourselves addressing the same problematic behaviours over and over, we may need to dig deeper to the thinking and feeling that drives those behaviours.'

One of my coaching clients put it perfectly when she said that not giving teammates honest feedback was 'like letting someone walk around with food in their teeth, and everyone knows, but no one says anything!' So if you're grappling with whether or not to provide feedback to someone, just think, am I letting them walk around with food in their teeth?

You don't need all the answers

Another challenge where leader courage is required is the need always to be right and know all the answers. During this time of great uncertainty, no one can know all the answers – it's impossible! You're putting a huge amount of unnecessary pressure on yourself if you think you need to be on top of everything all the time. Emotional courage is admitting you don't know all the answers and can be a gift to yourself and your team. On-going uncertainty is an opportunity to build trust, and research shows that asking for help is the number one way to do so. It also assists with performance.

Simon asked me to facilitate a workshop session for his leadership team to discuss how to best support their staff to transition back to the office. By getting his leadership team together to discuss these issues, Simon is asking for help and signalling that he doesn't know all the answers. It's emotional courage in action.

Reflection questions

What resonated with you in this chapter?

What insights do you have about your leadership?

What could you cultivate (grow more of)?

What could you eliminate (do less of)?

If you did this, how would your life be different?

If you did this, who else would benefit?

How would they benefit?

If you don't make a change, what are the consequences?

THE FIFTH KEY: A Cultivating Leader Connects

'Only through our connectedness with others can we really know and enhance the self. And only through working on the self can we begin to enhance our connectedness to others.'

Harrier Lerner

(Lerner, 1985)

Bridge the gap

Microsoft's annual *2021 Work Trend Index* report warned that business leaders are 'out of touch with employees and need a wake-up call'. The report found high levels of overwork and exhaustion among employees, but there was a major disconnect between their experience and their managers'.

Some sixty-one per cent of business leaders say they are thriving. That's twenty-three per cent more than their employees who have no decision-making authority. Leaders also report that they are building stronger relationships with colleagues and leadership, earning higher incomes and that they're taking all, or more, of their allotted vacation days (Microsoft, 2021).

This tallies with Dr Michelle McQuaid's research on well-being at work, which found that 'workers in job roles with more autonomy (C-level, owners, directors) continued to be more likely to report they were consistently thriving, while those with less autonomy (e.g. unskilled workers) were more likely to be struggling.' Also, 'leaders were statistically more likely to report higher levels of well-being ability, motivation and psychological safety than their team members' (The Well-Being Lab, 2021).

A cultivating leader continually connects with their employees to stay grounded and listen to their issues – they actively try to keep the hierarchy open – from leaders to the front line and back again. They have empathy and try to stand in the shoes of their people.

One of my clients, a cultivating leader called Matt, talked about how easy it can be for leaders to lose touch with staff's day-to-day lives and realities. He likened his team to the front line in battle. In the trenches, often in hand-to-hand combat, while people like him, further up the hierarchy, are removed, sitting in the comforts of the war room. He said that unless leaders are mindful and truly listen and understand staff experiences, they can forget what it is like to be in the trenches.

In his role, Matt might talk to company stakeholders directly twice a day, and his regional managers might take five calls a day. But the staff in the field, whose role is the direct liaison between the company and its suppliers, might be getting twenty to thirty calls a day, and they are out on farms visiting and talking to farmers directly. That is OK when things are going well in the industry, but when they aren't, with low prices and farmers in geographic areas dealing with events like floods or drought, his front-line staff are under relentless stress.

Another team that works in agriculture said their senior leaders were often dismissive of staff concerns. They invalidate them, think they are whinging and believe they need to be more resilient and just get on with things. This is empathy blockage, where the leaders aren't seeking to stand in the shoes of their employees. They have any lost awareness that their employees' experiences are different from theirs.

Dr McQuaid's research also showed the profound impact that a leader's behaviour has on the well-being and performance of employees. She found that if you have a leader who encourages you to look for new possibilities, role models this behaviour and can perceive the positive in situations, you are more likely to be more satisfied with your current life and have high well-being levels in the future. Having a leader who frequently expresses care, compassion and appreciation, increases your likelihood of:

- higher well-being, job satisfaction and workplace commitment
- thriving or living well despite the struggle
- feeling and performing better at work.

On the flip side, Gallup found (in the USA and Germany) that employees with a lousy manager had worse well-being than unemployed people (Gallup, 2021).

Dr McQuaid also said that leaders often thought they were doing an excellent job of checking in with staff, but staff wanted them to do it more often.

Look for support

The leader is like the pilot of a plane, trained to manage four levels of turbulence so that the plane (your organisation or business) and the passengers (your team and clients/stakeholders) can have the smoothest flight possible, despite the conditions.

Turbulence is classified as either light, moderate, severe or extreme. Different countries and sectors of the economy are currently operating in one of these four conditions.

One strategy that pilots use to navigate is to receive 'ride reports' from other aircrews that have encountered rough air. They also have a robust network of weather experts, air traffic controllers and other pilots working together to find smooth air.

As a leader, it's important to keep connected with others and get support. You don't have to do it all on your own. Humans are hardwired to connect with others, so keep reaching out to your network – especially when you might want to go inward.

As well as staying connected, your role is to help your team maintain their connections, collaboration and engagement. This is within and outside the team, such as customers, stakeholders and other teams.

Socially connected leaders encourage team members to connect with themselves under stress to improve self-awareness and personal growth.

Reflection questions

What resonated with you in this chapter?

What insights do you have about your leadership?

What could you cultivate (grow more of)?

What could you eliminate (do less of)?

If you did this, how would your life be different?

If you did this, who else would benefit?

How would they benefit?

If you don't make a change, what are the consequences?

THE SIXTH KEY:

A Cultivating Leader Encourages Accountability

'Elder Judy Atkinson is a world-leading expert in Indigenous trauma and recovery who has written a book about trauma called Song Lines. She said it's not our job to rescue people. It's our job to create safe spaces for people to be able to rescue themselves because you disempower people by trying to rescue them.'

Shantelle Thompson

(Thompson, 2020)

Step up

Jo is the chief financial officer of a business where I'd done a lot of work with the leadership team and staff on values and behaviours. Jo is dedicated, courageous and prepared to put into practice what she learnt during the program. One area on which she wanted to focus was having accountability conversations with some of her employees. It was something Jo felt she hadn't mastered. We talked through a structure for courageous conversations, then she prepared and practised what she was going to say and gave it a go.

Jo said, 'I was nervous the first time I did it, but now I've realised, really, it's not that hard, is it? It's not that hard to have an honest accountability conversation with someone.

> It's not that hard to have an honest accountability conversation with someone.

'Now, if I feel like someone is not taking responsibility for their role, I have a discussion with them. I prepare and ask questions to understand what happened and why. I make it clear that it's not a problem – I will never judge you negatively or think you are failing if you tell me early. We just need to understand why this has happened. If something is going wrong, if someone in the business is not giving you what you need, or a system is letting you down, you need to tell me straight away so I can help you. I've got your back. But I can't help you if you don't tell me.

'I've let my staff know that I don't care about mistakes. Let's just fix it and learn so we don't do it again. Sometimes you don't know what's important until a mistake is made.

'They know the boundaries of what I expect, and they know I trust them. I've told them, "I can't be checking your work all the time. I trust you to do it. Let's just keep the conversation going. I expect you to meet timelines and keep it all moving forward. I want you to own it. If you see better ways of doing something, please tell me."

'Before, when I was avoiding having these accountability conversations, I found out things weren't on track when other teams reported that things weren't done. For example, one of my staff kept asking someone more senior in the business for information and was getting nothing back. He was really stressed about it but didn't let me know. He didn't meet his deadline. When we had an honest conversation and got to the root cause, I could support him by chasing up the other person and getting the information we needed.

'My staff really appreciate this approach. It says they are accountable, I trust them, they know the boundaries, and when to come to me. They get where I'm coming from, and it's a relief for them. They can work autonomously and know that they are not getting checked up on by me. However, I do get grumpy if they don't do what they've promised and don't talk to me, because it's important that we deliver to our internal clients. If we show we address any problems or feedback, we show other teams that we get it.

'We've had conversations about the implications of not delivering on our word – it's that people can't trust us and we aren't doing our job. I say to my staff that I don't want you to be sorry, I want to work with you to fix it, and it's your responsibility. I write an email afterwards saying this is what we agreed.'

Model accountability

Author and social scientist Joseph Grenny found that teams break down in performance roughly as follows:

- In the weakest teams, there is no accountability.
- In mediocre teams, bosses are the source of accountability.
- In great teams, peers manage most performance problems with one another (Grenny, 2014).

A cultivating leader treats all employees fairly, with clear standards around individual and team accountability. This drives greater innovation, trust, and productivity.

Leaders play a big part in actively shaping the behaviours of their team so that there is a culture of mutual accountability and the leader isn't left feeling like the school principal. The leader can check in with employees rather than checking up on them.

Cultivating leaders frequently talk with their staff about their responsibilities and progress. They don't save those critical conversations for once-a-year performance reviews. There are many ways to define and influence behaviour and encourage accountability, such as:

- Develop a behavioural framework with the team. Clearly define expectations about how the team operates – what behaviour is OK and what's not in this team?
- Ensure everyone knows what's acceptable and what they should be aspiring to
- Have regular conversations with each other about behaviours, not just tasks and results
- Develop skills in universal accountability. Anyone should

be able to hold anyone accountable if it is in the best interests of the team

- Encourage team members to talk immediately and respectfully to each other when problems arise.

Most importantly, leaders need to model the desired behaviours, set the standard, and encourage and accept feedback. If you want to cultivate accountability in your team, start with agreeing on the OK and not OK behaviours, then diligently follow them yourself.

Most importantly, leaders need to model the desired behaviours, set the standard, and encourage and accept feedback.

In my work with leaders and teams, it's easy for teams to identify the behaviours they'd like the team to implement. Which positive behaviours do they want to see more of? What negative behaviours do they want to see less of? If they acted like this ideal individually and as a team, the team would fly, and individuals would be happier and perform well. But it's the operationalising that gets difficult. They talk the talk, but it doesn't translate into the walk.

Do you have the ingredients to ensure you're cultivating accountability? As the model in figure 22 explains, you need a system, commitment and consequences. Let's unpack those elements.

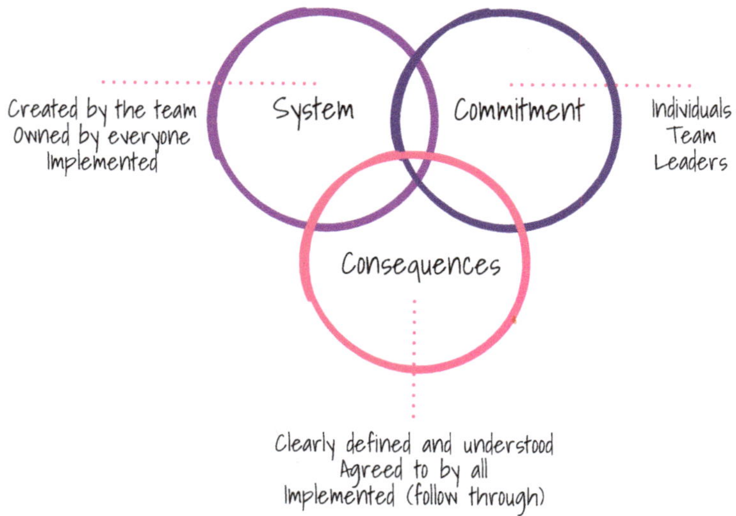

Figure 30: Embedding new team behaviours

A system

Once the team has identified the behaviours they'd like to embed, the next step is identifying the HOW. What's going to work for the team? What's your plan to implement your intended change or habit – when and where will you act?

We need to make it easy for people to take action. Therefore in our discussions about team behaviours, we also need to develop a system that individuals can follow.

This system needs to be created, owned and implemented by everyone in the team. It's up to you to lead and model it.

Without a system, it's like a football game where everyone is playing by different rules. In the same game, you might have someone playing AFL, someone playing soccer and someone playing rugby.

If we're all playing the same game, it's much easier to make progress around change.

Commitment

The second essential ingredient for embedding behaviour change in teams is commitment. It's essential at individual, group and leadership levels.

It's easy for people at a workshop or in a coaching session to say they commit to embedding new team behavioural standards and that they intend to implement them. I find they believe it at the time, but professed commitment is different to taking action, and this is where the best-laid plans go astray.

Any change starts with you. It's not up to anyone else to do this stuff and make the change; it's up to you! If all the individuals in the team truly commit to making a change, then this has flow-on effects for the whole team and organisation.

It's also crucial that the leadership group commits to change. Everyone will be watching and taking their cues from you. If you aren't serious, then the team won't be either. No one likes people who operate in 'do as I say, not as I do' mode. You can't ask someone to do something that you wouldn't do yourself.

So as a leader, how committed are you to doing the reflective and hard work of looking at yourself and changing yourself first?

I urge leaders not to take their teams through team-building or behaviour-change programs unless they are truly committed to doing the work themselves. Otherwise, you will simply build cynicism and destroy trust between the team and yourselves.

Consequences

The third essential element for embedding behaviour change in your team is consequences.

Team members have identified and agreed on the productive behaviours they'd like to see more of and the unproductive behaviours they'd like to see less of. They've developed a system together that supports the implementation of the behaviours they want to make. Everyone has committed to making the change.

And then someone doesn't do what you all agreed to.

If you want to undermine all the good work the team has done up to this point, you will tolerate this poor behaviour, and there will be no consequences for anyone who doesn't behave as you all agreed.

Most of us don't like conflict, so we often go into denial mode or try to rationalise bad behaviour rather than deal with it. If you, as a teammate or leader, convince yourself that it's not important, or believe that it will sort itself out, then you're part of the problem.

If someone breaks the rules during a game, they'll be removed from the ground for a time and perhaps face sanctions later. There might also be a reward for doing the right thing. There are clear positive and negative consequences for players that help reinforce behavioural standards.

What might work for your team? As part of the process, the team needs to discuss and agree on key consequences that are clearly defined and understood. Following through could be as a teammate or as a leader.

We're all only human so, of course, there will be times when we stuff up, don't do our best or choose to do something different.

Team performance is more of an art than a science – there needs to be give-and-take and some flexibility in any system.

Getting these three ingredients for success right will help you at an individual, team and leadership level with:

- Being consistent
- Developing transparency around behaviours with no surprises
- Establishing clear expectations
- Having everyone playing by the same rules with no double standards
- Building trust between team members and between the team and leaders
- Sticking to your commitments
- Learning from your mistakes
- Asking questions to dig deeper and understand why people may not have stuck with what they agreed to
- Developing the practice of personal reflection and your ability to achieve change
- Practising accountability and giving and receiving feedback
- Supporting individuals and the team to reach higher levels of performance in a productive and happier work environment.

Reflection questions

What resonated with you in this chapter?

What insights do you have about your leadership?

What could you cultivate (grow more of)?

What could you eliminate (do less of)?

If you did this, how would your life be different?

If you did this, who else would benefit?

How would they benefit?

If you don't make a change, what are the consequences?

PART FOUR

A Cultivating Culture

'Culture can be a by-product, or it can be an intention. Make no mistake, culture arrives whether you invited it or not. The big question is, do you like what shows up? The best cultures are intentional.'

Darren Hill

(Hill, 2021)

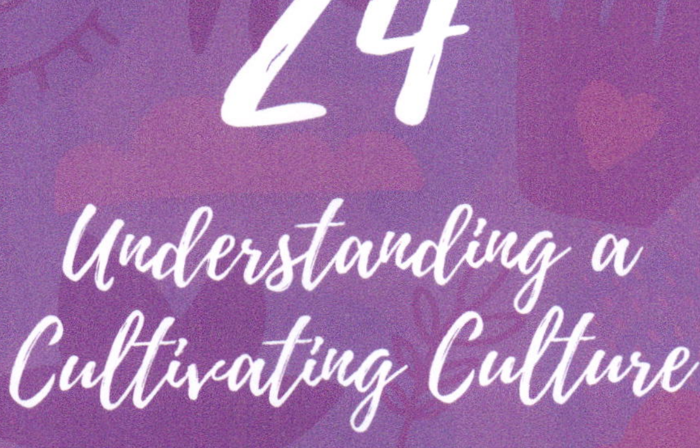

24

Understanding a Cultivating Culture

'Culture has more influence on an organisation's performance than strategy. Strategy is important but aligning the culture to the strategy is even more important. Culture belongs to people, not the organisation.'

Michael Henderson

(Henderson, 2014)

Recognise the need for change

Nadia is the CEO of a regional not-for-profit. She had been in the role for about a year when she contacted me after we met at a Brené Brown seminar. Along with four thousand other participants, we'd been in awe of Brené's research, wisdom and practical advice for being a courageous leader.

Hearing Brené talk about building courageous cultures through vulnerability crystallised in Nadia a need for culture change within her organisation. A couple of key staff members wielded power in the culture she had inherited. They were not open to change and displayed cynicism, judgement and a lack of respect for Nadia and others in the workplace. This created a lack of trust and safety that permeated the whole organisation. Staff members dreaded coming to work, and were afraid to speak up, and Nadia felt disempowered about leading culture change.

We developed a three-stage workshop program to build understanding and trust within the team. I worked with them to identify and name positive team norms that supported a strong, positive, shared culture.

The influential hostile staff members attempted to derail the first workshop. I don't think it was conscious or deliberate, but they made it difficult for Nadia and the other leaders to contribute to the conversations. Despite this, over several weeks, we heard from everyone about the type of organisation they wanted to be part of. This gave Nadia the confidence and backing to embed the culture change and have courageous conversations with her staff.

They were able to gain clarity about the importance of staff feeling safe, trusting each other and being willing to talk about the future. Interestingly, the three unaligned staff members chose to leave once the organisational behaviours and values were agreed on. Nadia and her leadership team recruited new staff aligned to the values and were very clear about what was expected when joining the team.

Nadia said, 'At the beginning of this work on our culture, it was really foggy and hard to work out exactly what was going on. There was just a feeling that it wasn't good. Now looking back, I can see that we've been able to go from a culture of fear and deficit to one full of possibility. We are clear about our culture and how to operationalise our values right across the whole organisation, including the board.

'We invested in this transformational work, and it allowed us to build more trusting relationships. We are also more grounded because we have done so much work on our personal and organisational values and how they align. It's one thing to say you work in line with your values and quite another to show up to them. We can now look at new projects and opportunities and ask if they align with our values before making a decision.'

Understand culture

Imagine a seed planted in soil. The gardener tends the seed with water and nutrition. As it grows, the gardener prunes, trains, and harvests the fruit. The seed's development and growth is affected by greater forces, such as sun, rain, disease and frost. If the seed represents a self-cultivated individual, and the gardener is the cultivating leader, then the bigger forces at play are the organisational culture.

It doesn't matter how good the seed or how well the gardener looks after its growth and development (the micro-environment). If the macro-environment is negative, harmful or toxic, the seed won't develop or flourish to its potential.

Now imagine there's not just one seed, but a variety of plants growing together, each unique and playing their part in a whole garden. The conditions of the macro-environment have a significant influence on whether the entire garden flourishes or struggles.

So how would you describe your macro-climate? I hope it's cultivated. The best way to know is to ask: Would I want someone I love or care about working here – in this workplace or this industry?

The best way to know is to ask: Would I want someone I love or care about working here – in this workplace or this industry?

If the answer is yes, then you have a cultivated culture. If the answer is no, then perhaps you don't.

Many of my clients don't work in such a positive environment. Their micro-climate might include working with a team of good people, doing good work alongside a good line manager, but above this, the organisation's culture isn't supportive.

One coaching client described her experience of workplace culture: 'The system is broken – we need to reboot and rejig it so that we look after people. We need to humanise a dehumanised system.'

Culture can be hard to pin down. There are many definitions, but these struck home for me: 'Culture is the patterns of behaviour that are encouraged, discouraged and tolerated by people and systems over time.' (Taylor, 2021). It's the cumulative effect of what people do and how they do it. It includes shared beliefs, values, behavioural norms, thinking and emotional intelligence; routines; and traditions of the organisation (Wilkinson, 2017).

Culture has two elements – cognitive and emotional. Many organisations focus primarily on cognitive culture, which is how we think and behave at work via intellectual values, norms and assumptions. Emotional culture dictates which emotions people have and express at work and which they believe they are better off suppressing (Barsade & O'Neill, 2016).

Emotional culture is created when senior leaders verbalise, model and reward the emotions they want in the organisation. That flows through to the next layer of management, which transmits these emotional signals to their employees. Emotional culture is often not managed as intentionally as cognitive culture, and a gap can form between the culture an organisation claims and how people within the organisation actually experience it. This typically plays out when people don't walk the talk.

That is why self-awareness and emotional courage are so crucial to business success. We need leaders who can articulate their emotions and feelings, and are willing to be vulnerable enough to do so. Research has shown that when leaders avoid discussing emotions, there is a cost to the organisation in the form of burnout, employee satisfaction, absenteeism, and financial and team performance. Addressing emotional culture means you recognise that your workplaces are full of humans, not machines.

I've identified three critical elements of a cultivating culture.

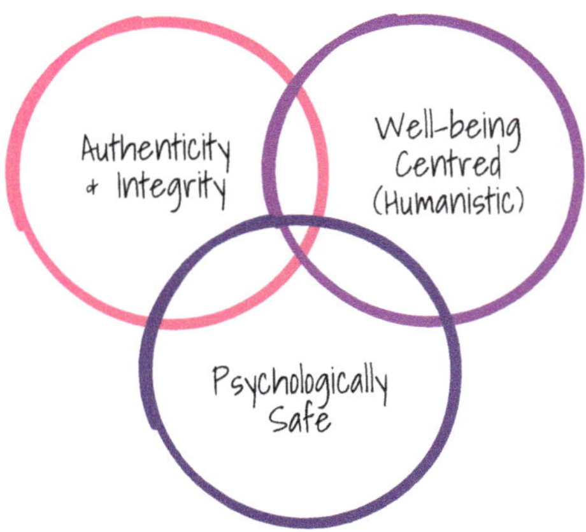

Figure 31: Three elements of a cultivating culture

A cultivating culture is like the root system of a plant that supports everything else to thrive. Get your culture right and see what else grows from this.

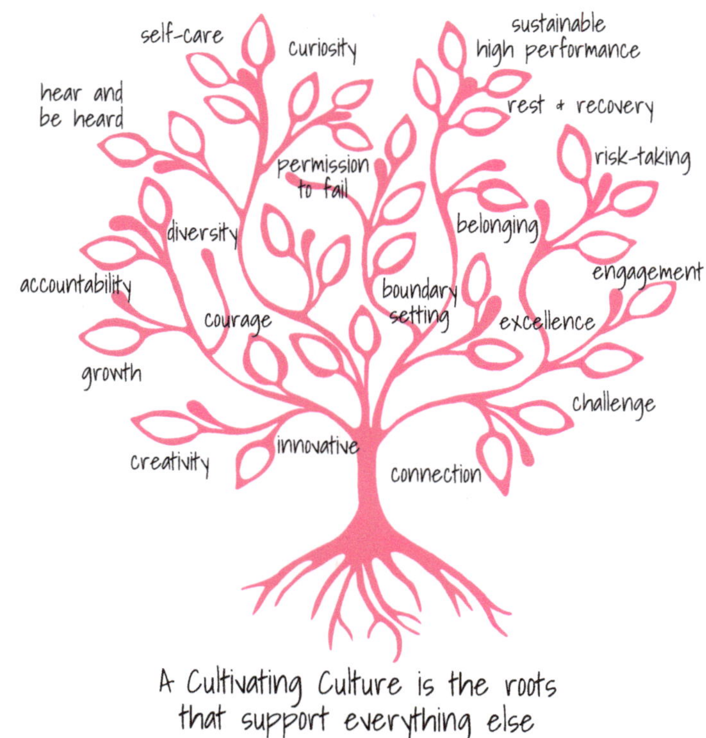

Figure 32: Cultivating culture supports growth

Reflection questions

What resonated with you in this chapter?

What insights do you have about your organisation/ industry/community culture?

What could you cultivate (grow more of)?

What could you eliminate (do less of)?

If you did this, how would your life be different?

If you did this, who else would benefit?

How would they benefit?

If you don't make a change, what are the consequences?

25 A Cultivating Culture is Psychologically Safe

'The individual has always had to struggle to keep from being overwhelmed by the tribe. If you try it, you will be lonely often, and sometimes frightened. But no price is too high to pay for the privilege of owning yourself.'

Rudyard Kipling

(Gordon, 1935)

Free to be ourselves

For years I wanted to be free to be me. To spread my wings and soar. To be my best and express myself fully. To dream and create. To be more and make a positive difference in the world.

But the organisational culture in which I was operating didn't seem to want the same things. It wanted me to be small. Not to make a rumble, just keep my head down and be less than myself. Not create trouble, question or challenge, but clip my wings to fit into a box. It expected me to be ordinary, middling and unremarkable. Being myself was offensive and wrong. I still performed, but I certainly didn't thrive, and there's a big difference.

For a long time, I took this as my fault. My self-esteem plummeted; I lost confidence, forgot who I was, and felt stuck and totally on my own. I was ashamed, afraid of upsetting people and getting into trouble and offending people. What was wrong with me? Why couldn't I fit in?

When you're constantly afraid to be yourself, going to work can feel like going to war. You take a deep breath and try to prepare for someone to derail you. To stay out of trouble, you hide. You second-guess yourself and never feel safe. Your career feels like it's built on quicksand. No matter how hard you work or how good your reputation is, it can all disappear in an instant if someone decides they don't like you. That means you're always looking over your shoulder. It's exhausting, demoralising, takes a huge toll on your confidence, saps your sense of self-worth, and

When you're constantly afraid to be yourself, going to work can feel like going to war.

is detrimental to your mental health and well-being. It has a financial cost, your career stalls, and it seeps into your personal life and affects those you love.

I've learned that trying to fit in and hide is called masking. Thirty-two per cent of employees who need to mask their behaviour at work say it has negatively impacted their sense of self. Masking is demotivating and negatively affects engagement. Research by Deloitte and Professor Kenji Yoshino from New York University found that employees who need to mask are sixteen per cent less committed to the organisation. They have a fourteen per cent lower sense of belonging and are fifteen per cent less likely to perceive having opportunities to advance. They are twenty-seven per cent more likely to have considered leaving the organisation in the past twelve months (Deloitte, 2019).

The organisational culture in which I operated for many years was psychologically unsafe.

It's inhuman. Many of us are like the walking wounded – with psychological battle scars and wounds that bleed into the rest of our lives and can continue to play out years later. Job insecurity, work overload, low role clarity, bullying and harassment, high or low job demands, low job control, poor support, poor workplace relationships, workplace violence, poor environmental conditions, poor organisational change management, low recognition and reward, poor organisational justice, remote or isolated work, violent or traumatic events, dealing with difficult customers, and shift work. These are common causes of workplace stress that lead to psychological injury (Stephens, 2018), (Safe Work Australia, 2019).

Dr Peta Miller, special adviser for Safe Work Australia, says that 'Poor psychological safety costs Australian organisations $6 billion per annum in lost productivity. This is primarily because psychological injuries require three times more time off work than other injuries. Additionally, workplaces with poor psychological working conditions accrue forty-three per cent more sick days per month' (Australian Network on Disability, 2018).

Why psychological safety matters

Google undertook rigorous research to find out what makes some teams succeed while others struggle. In 2012 they initiated Project Aristotle to study hundreds of Google teams across the world. The company's top executives hypothesised that if they combined the best and brightest people, they would create the highest performing teams.

It turned out that this wasn't the case. When the researchers analysed the data, they found that who was in the team didn't seem to matter. There was no evidence that a mix of specific personality types or skills, or backgrounds influenced team performance.

So, if it didn't matter who, what did influence team performance and success? The Google team started looking at how teams worked together and tapped into research that studied group norms. These are behavioural standards and unwritten rules that govern how we function when we are together.

They found that having the right norms in a team raised team IQ while having the wrong norms impeded a team – even if all members were very intelligent individually.

The Project Aristotle team knew that their high-performing teams had strong group norms, but they all seemed different. Some groups said that teammates interrupted one another constantly, while others politely waited for people to have their turn. Some successful teams celebrated birthdays and caught up on what was going on in each other's lives at the start of a meeting, whereas others got straight to business in meetings (Google, 2021).

Eventually, the Project Aristotle team discovered the work of Dr Amy Edmondson on psychological safety. She defined it as 'a sense of confidence that the team will not embarrass, reject or punish someone for speaking up'. The team climate is characterised by interpersonal trust and mutual respect in which people are comfortable being themselves (Edmondson, 2019).

This was a lightbulb moment for the Project Aristotle team.

They eventually realised that the teams with high rates of psychological safety were better than other teams at implementing diverse ideas and driving high performance. Team members were also more likely to stay with the company.

Psychologically safe team members felt comfortable to be themselves – they did not have to put on a work face or leave part of their personality and inner life at home to fit in and survive. Trust created psychological safety, increased the collective intelligence of the group and led to improved performance.

Trust created psychological safety, increased the collective intelligence of the group and led to improved performance.

Dr Emondson's research found that frontline staff generally feel less psychologically safe than higher-level employees. It's yet another example of how easy it is for leaders to become disconnected from the experiences and realities of their staff. Power dynamics also impact how safe someone feels. If we perceive we have lower status or power than someone else, we can experience fear. Edmondson says, 'Research in neuroscience shows that fear consumes cognitive resources, diverting them from parts of the brain that process new information. When experiencing fear, we are less able to engage in analytic thinking, creative insight and problem-solving. In short, it's hard for people to do their best work when they are afraid' (Caprino, 2018).

Create your own cultivating culture

Only when I took time off and stepped out of the environment could I reconnect with who I really am. I got myself back and realised I am usually a happy person. Eventually, this gave me the confidence to leave the organisation and start my own business.

Finding (or, in my case, creating my own) a cultivating culture where you are safe and love coming to work can be life-changing.

I believe that just as workplaces evolved to place a huge emphasis on employee physical safety, we are starting to see an equal need to ensure our workplaces and industries are psychologically safe.

Quad bikes and tractors were not originally built with roller bars, but because of high levels of workplace injury and death, legislation has been introduced, safety features enhanced, and education campaigns developed to improve physical workplace safety.

Worksafe has a section on its website called Tractor Rollover Protection Structures (ROPS) – Requirements. How to reduce or eliminate the risk of serious injury or death caused by tractor rollover through the correct selection and management of tractor rollover protection structures' (Worksafe, 2017). Our workplaces, organisational and industry cultures have evolved to have a safety-first culture, and those who don't embrace this are increasingly on the outer.

It is totally bonkers that workplaces are making people sick. Surely, then, the next step is to put rollover protection structures on human mental health, so we don't burn out and fall over.

Extensive research has found that rural Australians 'hold negative attitudes towards seeking professional help for physical and psychological illness and engage in more risk-taking behaviour. The higher prevalence of depression in rural workers is significant considering the negative impact that depression has on workplace productivity and the associated increased risk of suicide (Dollard, et al., 2012). The research found that the cost of implementing proactive strategies to reduce depression, such as mental health first aid, would be significantly less than treating depression once it manifested. The authors recommended that from a cost-effectiveness perspective, rural employers should consider these strategies first. For example, compared to their non-farming rural counterparts, Australian farmers are half as likely to have visited a GP or mental health worker in the prior twelve months.

Several researchers have suggested that rural populations rely more on community values, collective coping mechanisms and social cohesion when dealing with stress. That compares with metropolitan populations who rely more heavily on individualistic values and coping mechanisms (Caldwell & Boyd, 2009).

That leaves plenty of room for improvement in building trust and creating psychological safety in our workplaces, particularly the rural ones.

No brilliant jerks

Netflix has put much work into clearly defining the values, specific behaviours and skills they want to see in their business, so their emotional culture is one where people feel safe to perform at their best.

This is one of my favourite Netflix principles. 'On a dream team, there are no "brilliant jerks". The cost to teamwork is just too high. Our view is that brilliant people are also capable of decent human interactions, and we insist upon that. When highly capable people work together in a collaborative context, they inspire each other to be more creative, more productive and ultimately more successful as a team than they could be as a collection of individuals. The real values of a firm are shown by who gets rewarded or let go' (Netflix, 2021).

Brilliant jerks aren't worth it, and cultivating cultures don't tolerate or reward them, even if they sell or deliver more. Their effect on the culture and other staff is toxic. They are like a noxious weed that spreads and dampens the growth of the plants around them.

Showing up with civility

As we discussed earlier in the book, Christine Porath has studied the effects of civility in the workplace. In her 2018 TED talk, she explained that Israeli researchers have shown that medical teams exposed to rudeness perform worse in their diagnostics and in all their procedures. Teams exposed to rudeness didn't share information as readily and stopped seeking help from their teammates.

Porath added that her research shows, 'When we have more civil environments, we're more productive, creative, helpful, happy and healthy. Civility lifts people. Incivility chips away at people and their performance. It robs people of their potential, even if they're just working around it. We can do better.'

We can disrupt ourselves and increase our civility levels by asking ourselves this one question. In every interaction, we ask, 'Who do I want to be?' Emotions are infectious, and checking through this simple question can have an incredible positive ripple effect on everyone around us.

> We can disrupt ourselves and increase our civility levels by asking ourselves this one question. In every interaction, we ask, 'Who do I want to be?'

Another study she was involved in found that participants who were treated rudely by other subjects were thirty per cent less creative than others in the study. They produced twenty-five per cent fewer ideas, and the ones they did come up with were less original (Porath, 2019).

What about your culture? Is it civil? Is it safe? Do you tolerate brilliant jerks? As a leader, how do you create psychological safety and build trust? What are your cultural norms? Are they healthy or unhealthy? What do people feel they can say, and what don't they talk about? Do you deliberately set the emotional and the cognitive culture, or is it left up to chance?

Reflection questions

What resonated with you in this chapter?

What insights do you have about your organisation/ industry/community culture?

What could you cultivate (grow more of)?

What could you eliminate (do less of)?

If you did this, how would your life be different?

If you did this, who else would benefit?

How would they benefit?

If you don't make a change, what are the consequences?

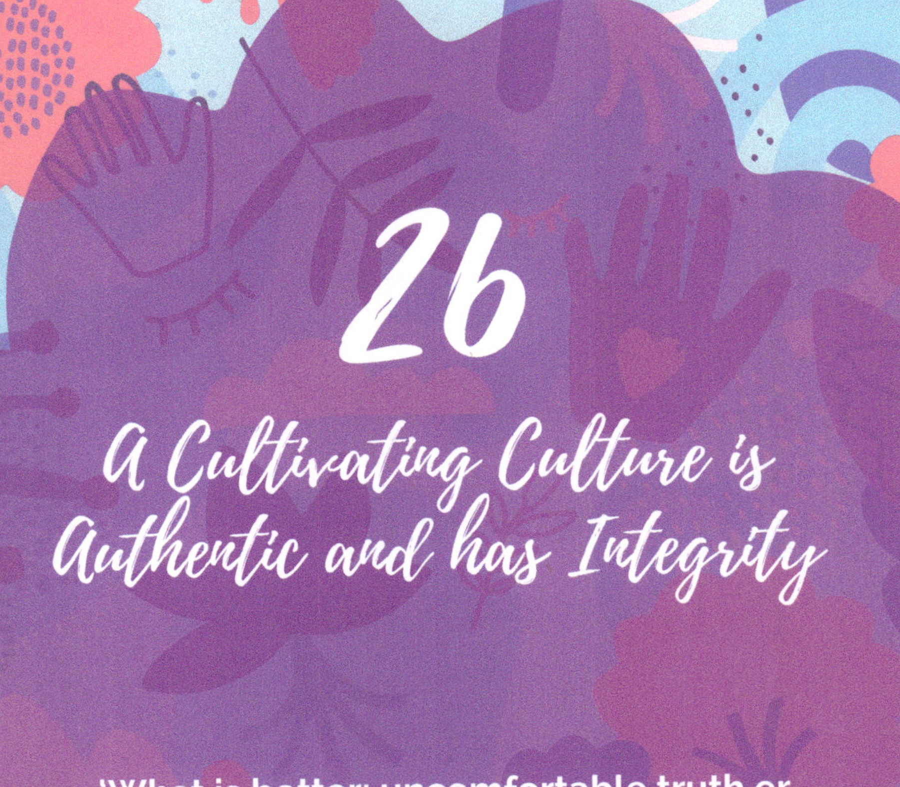

26

A Cultivating Culture is Authentic and has Integrity

'What is better: uncomfortable truth or comfortable lies? Every truth is a kindness, even if it makes others uncomfortable. Every untruth is an unkindness, even if it makes others comfortable.'

Glennon Doyle

(Doyle, 2020)

Look to your role models

One of the most authentic leaders I've experienced in my working life was Dr Chloe Munroe. She was secretary of the Department of Natural Resources and Environment (DNRE) back in the early 2000s. Why was she so outstanding? It was her direct impact on creating, leading and cultivating a positive, collaborative culture in our organisation.

As already discussed, it can be hard to pin down who is responsible for culture and how it is set. It can seem a bit nebulous and out of our direct control. As a young woman in my early career, I observed Chloe step into her role as secretary and implement a culture change program that deeply impacted staff.

Too often, culture is just left to happen, or we set organisational values (and sometimes behaviours), then we see the leaders who don't walk the talk, and it all rings hollow. No wonder people get cynical when values are not embraced or when they stay at the theoretical level in a strategic plan or on a website, and that's as far as it goes.

Values are only useful if they are operationalised and put into practice. Nadia, the CEO you met earlier, did this well, and Chloe did too. Leaders set the culture.

Chloe led a program called One NRE that brought several departments in the agriculture and natural resource space together under one umbrella. The idea was to improve relationships and communication and break down silos between groups working on similar issues but coming from different perspectives and policy aims.

Chloe communicated every week with staff via emails and videos that always referred to One NRE. In our region, facilitators were assigned to bring staff together from different branches to build relationships and have conversations about what One NRE could look like. The Regional Management team even experimented with a board structure with a rotating chair to share team leadership between the branches.

Chloe's message was consistent and clear. The program came from a place of authenticity. It was organised and coordinated with nothing left to chance. She put her credibility on the line and was prepared to take action and risks to implement it. Chloe built trust with staff through her communication.

The program was resourced with facilitators (I was one). The leaders in our region got on board and supported the program. People were engaged throughout all parts of the organisation. Even highly cynical staff in our region ended up embracing the program because it was clear it wasn't just words on paper, or meaningless jargon, or a flash in the pan. It was here to stay. (Note: Until it wasn't, when the government changed, the department split, and Chloe left.)

Chloe Munroe died in 2021. The words that family, colleagues and friends used to describe her were consistent. She radiated positive energy. She had a warm heart. She greeted everyone with characteristic glowing warmth. She was authentic. She connected with people and seeded connections between them. Chloe was an inspiring leader and an extraordinary person who could light up a room and energise people. She made everyone she talked to feel special. She cared for others and brought wisdom, governance, experience and calm humanity to our company.

People also said she led without controlling and delivered on her promises. She showed respect and curiosity in conversation while challenging you to be your best self. Chloe was bold, creative and agile. A disruptor, non-hierarchal and always present. Her ability to be charmingly honest, non-judgemental and thoughtful. The way she backed herself and her people made her a leader others wanted to follow. I will never forget her style, her smile and her bright lipstick. Our world is a better place because of Chloe.

More than twenty years after the days of One NRE, when friends from DNRE get together, we still talk about the program and Chloe. We recall that she was a great example of leadership and culture change. It was such a positive experience for us as staff members and young women working in a government organisation. That is both unusual and extraordinary. In nearly twenty years of working for the government, I can't recall another program that impacted the culture and truly made a positive difference.

Chloe left a tremendous legacy and a profound impact on so many people. She is my definition of a cultivating leader who set, led, and implemented a cultivating culture through her authenticity, integrity, heart, and courage.

Implementing a culture change program can be damaging if the leaders aren't serious about it or profess values that they don't live by. When authenticity and integrity are lacking, or a program is done to tick a box or look good, staff pick this up straight away. It destroys trust, leads to disengagement and cynicism. Morale and productivity suffer.

Often leaders can have good intentions about the culture they want to create, but it remains as theory and isn't operationalised effectively. Or it stays front of mind for a couple of months, then slides off the agenda. When it isn't reinforced, it doesn't become part of the DNA of the organisation or business.

As someone who worked many years in government (as did my Dad before me), I have seen many destructive and toxic organisational cultures develop despite the leaders' positive organisational values and good intentions.

The difference with One NRE was that Chloe Munroe truly believed, owned, led, supported, reinforced, resourced and implemented it over time. At least that's how it came across to us as staff members.

Walking the talk

Creating a culture of true authenticity and integrity requires leaders to walk the talk. Ralph Kellogg wrote, 'Authenticity feels scary because challenging the status quo requires leaders to turn the mirror on themselves and the organization and ask if established norms and behaviours have created a culture of authenticity or one of conformity' (Kellogg, 2020).

I recall an executive telling staff about a new set of organisational values. He said we had permission to call out anyone (including senior management) who wasn't living the values. As he went through the values, which included trust and respect, I looked around the room and saw all the staff had their heads down and arms crossed. The room was silent, the energy was low, and it looked like people wanted to be anywhere else than there. We had just been told our office was to close, and we would be moved to other locations. It was a controversial issue, and trust between staff and management was low. There was an elephant in the room that no one was talking about.

I took a deep breath and raised my hand to ask how the relocation process related to the values, as there seemed to be a disconnect. My intent was to open a door for the executive to address the elephant in the room and acknowledge what was really going on.

Instead of thanking me for my question and addressing it, the executive held up the glossy new pamphlet covered with the values and proceeded to scold me. Apparently, I was contravening the values by not showing him respect or trust. The message to the room was clear, 'I've given you permission to call me out on the values, but don't actually do so, or you will be publicly shamed.'

McKinsey research has shown that organisational and individual change are inseparable. Change efforts often falter because individuals overlook the need to make fundamental changes in themselves. They found that 'half of all efforts to transform organisational performance fail either because senior managers don't act as role models for change or because people in the organization defend the status quo.' In other words, despite the stated change goals, people on the ground tend to behave as they did before' (Boaz & Fox, 2014). That is why it is so essential for leaders to be prepared to lead the culture.

> Change efforts often falter because individuals overlook the need to make fundamental changes in themselves.

Trust is like a candle flame. It is quickly extinguished when people don't do what they say they will. An authentic culture with integrity requires a lot of work by its leaders – but it's worth it.

Instead of seeing staff with heads down and arms crossed, you look around, and they are engaged and attentive, with their heads up. People lean into each other and towards you. Instead of silence, you hear animated conversations, where ideas are exchanged, questions asked and explored. Instead of low energy, there is a great vibe in the room with people excited about being at work and high morale. Instead of elephants in the room and a lack of trust between leaders and staff and each other, people are willing to name issues, take emotional risks, be open. They have high trust and feel safe.

What you praise, call out, share, or ignore shapes the culture (Razzetti, 2019). Don't ask others to do what you are not prepared to do yourself. Make sure to have good people around who keep you honest and are ready to be courageous and provide you with grounding feedback. Listen, be curious, open and willing to change your mind. Don't view different opinions as challenges, but rather as opportunities to explore. If you make mistakes, own them, share them and use them as a learning and growth opportunity for all. You're human – you can't be perfect all the time. It's important that your staff know that their leaders make mistakes too.

Reflection questions

What resonated with you in this chapter?

What insights do you have about your organisation/ industry/community culture?

What could you cultivate (grow more of)?

What could you eliminate (do less of)?

If you did this, how would your life be different?

If you did this, who else would benefit?

How would they benefit?

If you don't make a change, what are the consequences?

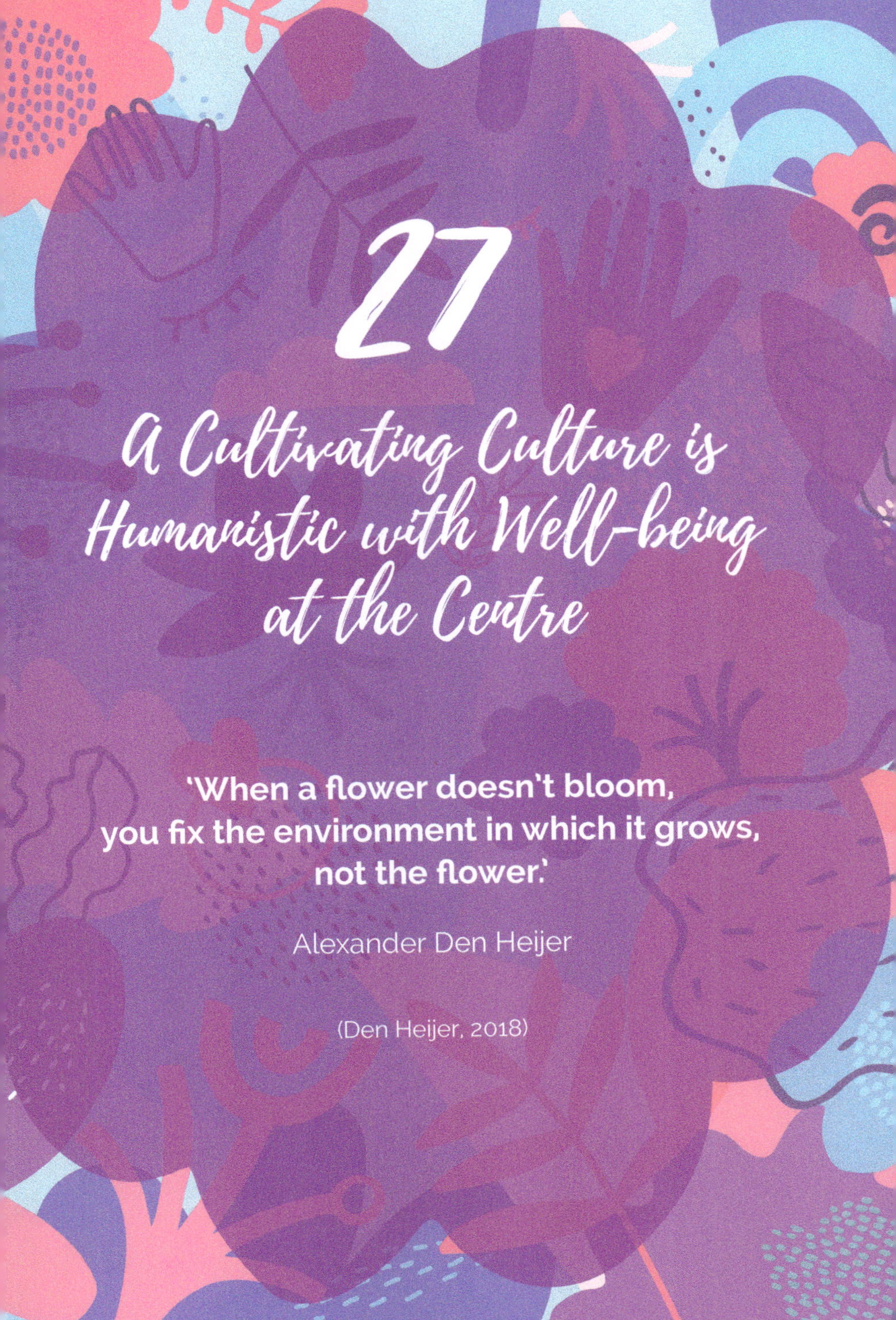

27

A Cultivating Culture is Humanistic with Well-being at the Centre

'When a flower doesn't bloom, you fix the environment in which it grows, not the flower.'

Alexander Den Heijer

(Den Heijer, 2018)

No band-aids for well-being

Sonja came to me because she was suffering burnout. She said, 'I told my manager, who is really lovely, that I wasn't coping as I had to do two additional roles on top of my substantive role and the workload was just too much, I was totally stressed and exhausted. He looked at me with sympathy and said, "I'm sorry, but you'll just have to keep going. There's no-one else to do the work."' Absolutely deflated, she walked away thinking, 'Right, I just have to suck this up.'

Two weeks later, Sonja drove to a meeting in another town and had a car accident. The police were called, and she ended up being charged with careless driving. She had to navigate the fallout on her own without any organisational support. Through twenty years of driving, she'd never had any kind of accident and only one speeding fine.

No amount of self-care could overcome the fact that the root cause of Sonja's burnout was the sheer workload required by the organisation. Getting a massage, deep breathing, meditation, nutrition, exercise, yoga – all these well-being strategies would have just been band-aids that were not addressing the underlying issue of a demanding work environment.

A worldwide survey conducted by Gallup found that seven in ten people worldwide are struggling and suffering in their lives (Gallup, 2021).

I see many people trying to develop strategies to deal with stress and overload. They have a courageous conversation with their manager to push back and set boundaries to look after themselves, only to find that the organisation's culture doesn't make this acceptable. Often this is despite public statements that looking after their employees is important. We have workshops where we talk about stress and well-being, then in the leadership group, there is a discussion about how it's detrimental to your career to push back from senior management's demands.

In many rural and regional teams and organisations, there are added responsibilities around emergency management like drought and fire, while others in the general workplace have now added emergency management (COVID-19) to their substantive role.

John is a team leader just below executive level in a state government organisation. In an interview, he said, 'I know having staff contributing to statewide emergency management is valuable and positive and makes a contribution to Victoria, but from my perspective, as a team manager, it just means I've got two people out of my team every week. The other team manager and I have chosen not to be involved (even though we'd like to, because it's a great development opportunity) because we can't manage. It would impact too negatively on our workload, our well-being and our team's well-being. COVID responsibilities have been in addition to our usual emergency management. I thought we were wrapping up, but now it's going on and on.

Whose responsibility is burnout?

'What can you keep tolerating? And when do you start saying no? As a manager, you need to balance your team's corporate responsibility against your responsibility for what you've got to deliver. And if you're not delivering, the responsibility gets put back on you. If you try to push back by saying our team is working on fire or COVID, which is affecting our ability to deliver, after a while, senior leadership say, "Oh, well, who cares? You still should be managing". It's seen as a personal failure.'

Christina Maslach is a professor of psychology at the University of California, Berkeley and a researcher at the school's Healthy

Workplaces Center. She says there is a common fallacy that burnout and stress are personal weaknesses or flaws, but they usually have to do with an unhealthy work environment rather than an individual unable to take care of themselves (Thorbecke, 2021).

People feel unable to push back – or if, like Sonja, they try to, the responsibility is put back on them as an individual to manage their own self-care. They just need to 'learn to be more resilient', 'be your best self', 'have a growth mindset', 'be more positive', 'manage your time better', 'be more high-performing', 'develop strategies to deal with your stress' and so on.

We already know that senior managers can be totally disconnected from the experience of frontline employees. Senior managers have much higher levels of well-being than their employees, so they are not in survival mode, just trying to get through each day.

A leadership consultant told me that the CEOs and senior managers she worked with were interested in high performance, while frontline workers were interested in how to balance work and life. You can't be high-performing if your well-being is low and stress levels are high. Forty-five per cent of Australian workers will experience a mental health condition in their lifetime, and every worker takes an average of three days off work each year due to stress (Australian Bureau of Statistics, 2007).

Ann Sherry, CEO of UNICEF Australia, is encouraging more workplaces in Australia to be certified family-friendly (through an Australia-first National Work and Family Standards). She says that many companies have really good workplace flexibility policies, but workers still feel that their careers can grind to a screaming halt if they use them. That's because they're seen as not committed enough. She wants to see organisations have the policies and implement them well (walk the talk), with all genders utilising them (Kelly, 2021).

One of my dear friends, Freya, works for the public service. She explained the incongruence between what organisations say and how that translates to the implementation reality for employees in a burn-out culture. 'We have pandemic leave which we are encouraged to take to help with the demands of homeschooling. My partner is an essential worker, so it's just been me at home trying to work full-time with two primary-school-aged children. It has been so hard. I am so stressed and feel I'm at breaking point. I'm thinking I might need to resign because I can't manage it.'

When I asked why she wasn't taking advantage of the pandemic leave policy, Freya said, 'If I take leave, then it ends up being even more stressful. Our workload is so high that if I take time off, I have to make it up later to deliver what they still expect. It's not like the workload reduces. It's not worth it.'

This was a great example of the bind many employees are in even though they are part of an organisation that says all the right things and probably has the best intentions about employee well-being. What they haven't done is renegotiated workloads to make it workable for staff to take leave. It ends up being an empty policy, and instead of creating a cultivating culture of well-being, it ends up being a high-performance culture of burnout masquerading as human-first. Talk about mixed signals for staff.

Address the underlying problems

I once rented an old house in the country that had cracks in the walls. Periodically the owner got the plasterer in to fill in the gaps, but eventually, they showed again. Once more, the owner would plaster and paint over them. The cracks didn't go away – the foundations of the building were still shifting.

I think a well-being culture is similar. If you put all the responsibility for self-care onto employees but don't do anything about the organisational well-being culture or put people first, then you're just plastering and painting over cracks in the wall. The cracks will still be there, and they will keep breaking through because you haven't addressed the structural problems.

> If you put all the responsibility for self-care onto employees but don't do anything about the organisational well-being culture or put people first, then you're just plastering and painting over cracks in the wall.

Dr Michelle McQuaid says that to support thriving, workplaces and communities must prioritise training, tools, and support to help people feel confident, committed, and connected. Do we enable our leaders to have regular conversations about well-being? Is well-being valued, embedded and measured in the workplace? Are people provided with the tools to explore well-being and what it looks like to them? Are the trust and psychological safety levels there to enable open conversations and for a staff member to admit they might be struggling? Is there permission for people to struggle at work and talk about it without judgement, punishment or for this to be a career-limiting move?

If we focus on developing cultivating cultures, well-being must be central to how they operate. Everyone will benefit, as the research shows that leaders who express appreciation and care for their staff are more likely to have high levels of personal well-being along with job performance, job satisfaction and workplace commitment (The Well-Being Lab, 2021).

I read a fabulous post on LinkedIn from Ian Sohn, president and chief client officer at Hawkeye. It showed the well-being and humanistic culture he is setting and leading at his organisation. In dismay, he wrote, 'I deeply resent how we've infantilized the workplace. How we feel we have to apologize for having lives. That we don't trust adults to make the right decision. How constant connectivity/availability (or even the perception of it) has become a valued skill.' He said, 'Years ago, a very senior colleague reacted with incredulity that I couldn't fly on twelve hours' notice because I had my kids that night (and I'm a single dad, edit: divorced). I didn't feel the least bit guilty, which I could tell really bothered said colleague. But it still felt horrible.'

He finished his post with this message to his staff, 'I never want you to feel horrible for being a human being.'

A cultivating culture is very freeing and allows us to bring our whole human being to work, which is so important because we're not robots. Our homes, lives and work environments aren't disconnected or separate – each impacts the other. One gift of the challenging pandemic has been more humanising of work and greater awareness of the impact of different people's circumstances and the importance of well-being.

Does your culture make people feel horrible or guilty for being human? Or does it accept that people will travel up and down the well-being ladder and support them no matter where they are?

Reflection questions

What resonated with you in this chapter?

What insights do you have about your organisation/ industry/community culture?

What could you cultivate (grow more of)?

What could you eliminate (do less of)?

If you did this, how would your life be different?

If you did this, who else would benefit?

How would they benefit?

If you don't make a change, what are the consequences?

Evolving from High Performance to Cultivating Cultures

'The way I think about culture is that modern humans have radically changed the way that they work and the way that they live. Companies need to change the way they manage and lead to match the way that modern humans actually work and live.'

Brian Halligan

(Nisen, 2013)

The cycle of culture

While writing this book, I've had the first few verses of The Byrds' song Turn! Turn! Turn! (To Everything There Is a Season) on constant play in my head (Seeger, 1965). I keep coming back to it when thinking about cultivating cultures because it perfectly articulates the reality of the cyclical nature, ebbs and flows and seasonality of the range of life experiences we have as human beings.

As the song goes:

> To everything, there is a season
> And a time to every purpose, under heaven
> A time to be born, a time to die
> A time to plant, a time to reap
> A time to kill, a time to heal
> A time to laugh, a time to weep
> To everything, there is a season
> And a time to every purpose, under heaven
> A time to build up, a time to break down
> A time to dance, a time to mourn
> A time to cast away stones, a time to gather stones together
> To everything, there is a season
> And a time to every purpose, under heaven

A cultivating culture is real. Where it is truly OK not to be OK, and you won't be punished or judged for being real. In Australia, there's a suicide prevention charity called R U OK? Its mission is to 'inspire and empower people to meaningfully connect with those in their world and lend support when they are struggling with life' (R U OK?, 2021).

Each year the organisation holds a day of action embraced by many workplaces called R U OK? Day. This event aims to build awareness of and skills in having conversations when people are struggling. It helps people understand what they can say and do to help someone feel supported and access appropriate help long before they're in crisis. To bring it back to the well-being ladder that is core to this book, R U OK? Day helps us intervene before people reach the lower rungs.

I love that we are having these conversations in our workplaces and, in doing so, removing the stigma from mental health, well-being and burnout issues. We have come a long way, but there is still much to do. I would like to think that the experiences of the pandemic will be a platform where we can evolve our organisational cultures to cultivating ones.

I was heartened when speaking with a human resources manager of a national horticulture business. She said, 'For us, it has been business as usual over the pandemic in many ways, but I've noticed our staff are much more aware of each other's personal circumstances.' For example, 'I'm not going to get grumpy if I have to pick up a bit of slack for you at the moment because I know you have three kids at home under ten and are having to do home-schooling.' She said, 'I hope we can continue to take this attitude forward'.

Evolution and revolution

For the pragmatists amongst us, it makes sound business sense to evolve to a cultivating culture. Recent research reported by McKinsey & Company found that employees are craving investment in the human aspects of work. Employees were far more likely to prioritise relational factors and meaningful interactions, whereas employers were more likely to focus on transactional ones.

Many employees are now looking to work at places that meet this need. They are shunning transactional cultures and voting with

> Employees were far more likely to prioritise relational factors and meaningful interactions, whereas employers were more likely to focus on transactional ones.

their feet. The McKinsey researchers termed the effect of this 'The Great Attrition'. Across a range of industries in Australia, Canada, Singapore, the United Kingdom, and the United States, they found forty per cent of employees surveyed said they are at least somewhat likely to quit in the next three to six months. Eighteen per cent said their intentions range from likely to almost certain. Imagine losing between twenty and forty per cent of your workforce? That is a huge cost, disruption and risk to your business.

The McKinsey report also found that many employers don't understand what their employees truly value. 'By not understanding what their employees are running from, and what they might gravitate to, company leaders are putting their very businesses at risk' (de Smet, Dowling, Mugayar-Baldocchi, & Schaninger, 2021).

Top three reasons why employees quit an organisation	**Top three reasons why employers thought employees quit**
Didn't feel valued by their organisations (54%)	Compensation
Didn't feel valued by their managers (52%)	Work-life balance
Didn't feel a sense of belonging at work (51%).	Poor physical and emotional health

Table 1: Disconnect between employees and employers

For many rural industries, where attracting and retaining labour is a huge issue, there is much to be learned about becoming an employer of choice by embracing a cultivating culture.

How do you evolve from a high-performance culture to a cultivating one? I think there are four steps to the change.

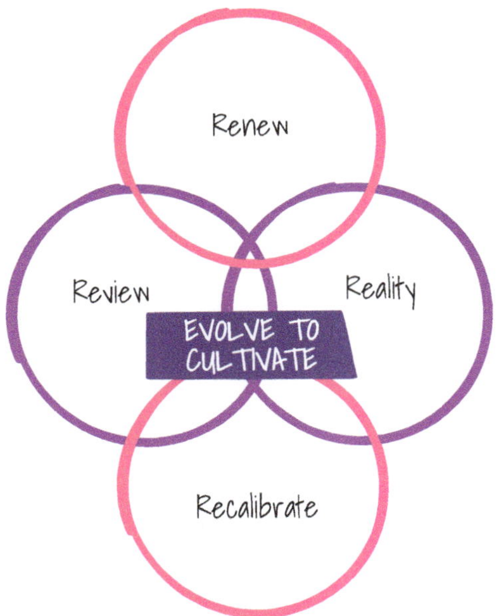

Figure 33: Evolving beyond high performance to well-being and human-centred

First, as leaders, we need to review and reflect on our expectations of the people in our workplaces and examine what it would look like to evolve beyond high performance to cultivating cultures. What is our culture like at the moment? How did we get here? What's contributing to it?

Then we acknowledge the reality of work and life – now and for the future – and talk about it within our teams. Be honest about the cost of burnout to our people and our businesses. Help people feel safe and let them know their well-being comes first.

The next step is to recalibrate expectations of individual and team performance. What does performance look like in a well-being and humanistic culture? What can we realistically expect? What's acceptable and what's not? How do we acknowledge the human element during this time and factor that into our expectations for work performance? What can we let go of that doesn't serve us anymore? What can we cultivate?

Throughout the book, we've talked about cultivation as a dynamic, ever-changing process of letting go, rest, renewal, and growth. The final stage of this evolution process is renewal, so you can create an environment of growth, and the new shoots can emerge for the cultivating culture and leadership you have created.

Reflection questions

What resonated with you in this chapter?

What insights do you have about your organisation/industry/community culture?

What could you cultivate (grow more of)?

What could you eliminate (do less of)?

If you did this, how would your life be different?

If you did this, who else would benefit?

How would they benefit?

If you don't make a change, what are the consequences?

Afterword

Rural leaders face massive pressures as they are embedded in their communities and constantly interact with people they work with. They see the consequences of their decisions every day. They are completely visible.

Rural communities have struggled with drought, fires, floods and COVID-19 for years. Mental health outcomes are poorer, and a tendency towards stoicism, particularly in men, can prevent honest conversations about challenges and how people are really coping. There is often pressure to keep up a front.

In rural and urban workplaces worldwide, there is a burnout epidemic. The ways of working that got us to this point need to be reinvented to reflect how we want to work and live. The pandemic has changed the place of work in our lives. A shift is here.

A more sustainable and real way of working recognises our humanity and puts well-being at the centre. It is what we need to embrace to effectively navigate this complex and rapidly changing world. I call this new way of working, Cultivate.

Cultivate is a process of nurturing, nourishing, fostering and refining. It's encouraging and improving through labour, care or study. Cultivate is relational rather than transactional. It's an organic process of ups and downs where it truly is OK not to be OK at work.

Where high performance philosophies have served us well, they are no longer fit-for-purpose. This is evident in the figures on burnout and employee engagement. The old ways of working don't reflect the reality of our current lives and how we want to live. Current workplace structures and cultures are outdated. They are like offering us Model-Ts when our goal is for everyone to drive an electric car.

High performance is an outcome, but when pursued as a strategy, it can become a self-defeating prophecy. People aren't machines, and our work and personal lives are intertwined. Issues that were previously taboo to talk about at work or viewed as unprofessional (depression, mental health, struggle, menopause) are no longer – thank goodness. Taboos constrain, whereas talking openly about what is going on with us frees us to bring our whole selves to work without the debilitating need to wear a mask or put on a show.

Cultivate is about the reality of being human and having good and bad days, months and years. Humans are messy. Life is messy. Let's live with it.

Neuroscience and modern leadership theories provide valuable insights and validation for why cultivate works. I want to help rural leaders develop this neuro-leadership superpower to make their leadership more effective and enjoyable for themselves, their staff and their organisations.

I hope this book has encouraged you to think about the process of cultivation through three lenses:

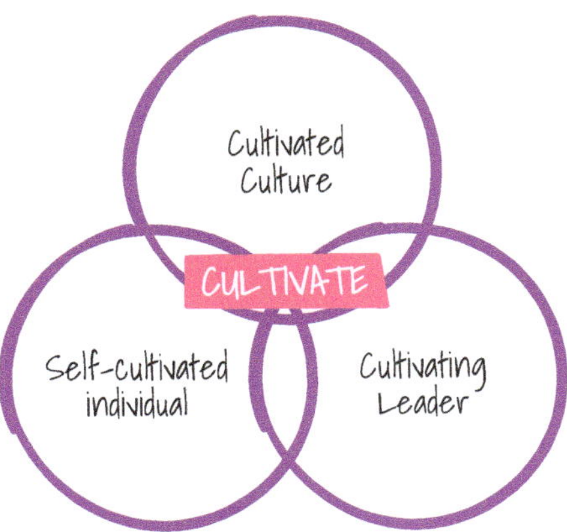

Figure 34: Three lenses of cultivation

Before leading others, lead yourself. This is the foundation of being a self-cultivated individual.

We are crying out for cultivating leaders who get the best from us while enabling us to be authentic.

Cultivated cultures are sustainable and human-centred and don't use well-being as a band-aid. They attract, engage, develop and retain employees by understanding their need for meaningful interactions and value relationships over transactions.

For more task-oriented and results-driven leaders, embracing a cultivating way can help you achieve your goals. If people are happy and their well-being is high, they will perform better. They will be more engaged.

People-focused leaders thrive in the cultivate model. But if you're struggling to motivate staff; encourage innovation; increase growth and profits; decrease staff turnover, absenteeism and presenteeism; reduce business risk; improve customer service; increase quality and improve efficiency, then a cultivating approach will set up the brain-friendly environment your staff need to be their best.

From small seeds, great things grow

I'd love you to sow the cultivate seeds amongst your network. Share the book, talk about the ideas, ask questions, listen to each other and explore the possibilities of what human-centred workplaces can look like. What would it mean to have more cultivating in your world?

If you see someone behaving as a cultivating leader, whatever their title, let them know what you value and the impact of their behaviour. Most importantly, start with small steps and apply what you've learnt to yourself.

I want people to understand and appreciate their own – and each other's – worth and value. By being more self-aware, courageous and compassionate (more relational and less transactional), I believe we can create workplaces and industries where people connect, belong, shine and are their best, most authentic selves. This has a flow-on effect in all aspects of our lives. When you look after yourself and are in a supportive, nurturing environment, you feel better. This, in turn, positively affects your colleagues. When you go home, your family gets the best of you, not what's left of you. The children in your life see a positive example when you set boundaries, look after yourself and are accountable for how you choose to show up at work and in life. You set the tone for the next generation. This is life-changing! It matters.

Together we can grow stronger, healthier and happier rural people, leaders, workplaces and communities. Environments in which you would want the people you love to live and work. Let's see what we can cultivate together!

To finish, it's appropriate to return to where we started this cultivating journey – to the immortal Dr Seuss and the final page of his wonderful book, Oh, the Places You'll Go (Seuss, 1990):

> *'So...*
> *Be your name Buxbaum or Bixby or Bray*
> *Or Mordecai Ali Van Allen O'Shea*
> *You're off to Great Places!*
> *Today is your day!*
> *Your mountain is waiting.*
> *So get on your way!'*

I can't wait to see how your cultivating journey unfolds. Good luck, enjoy the work, look after yourself, and happy travels!

How can I help?

I hope this book has inspired you to undertake some compassionate self-reflection and recognise the many fabulous things that you are already doing so well. Keep building on what is already working and leverage your strengths.

I also hope that it has raised questions you'd like to explore, piqued your curiosity about particular topics and enabled you to identify opportunities for further development and growth.

If you'd like to learn more about how to apply cultivation to yourself, your team, your organisation, industry or community, then let's talk about how we can work together.

All programs can be delivered virtually or face-to-face.

Cultivating You

I support the growth and development of a limited number of clients through one-on-one coaching and mentoring. In this process, I partner with you in the important work of asking powerful questions to provoke reflection and unlock new insights, perspectives and learnings that lie within. I provide the space and use coaching processes for you to dream big about your goals, create new ideas about what's possible and identify strategies to implement. I'm your accountability buddy, sharing experiences and tools to support you to do the work, take action and create change.

Cultivated Teams

Each year I offer tailored group programs that help teams cultivate trust and connection, undertake self-reflection, have honest conversations, and work together effectively and sustainably. These programs include half-day workshops, monthly masterclasses, and a twelve-month program involving teams across your whole organisation. My programs are based on the latest learnings from neuroscience and positive psychology, and are practical, interactive, fun, safe, supportive and highly effective.

Cultivated Leaders

I also work with leadership teams, individually and as a collective, to understand how they show up as leaders in shaping their organisational culture and leading their teams. I provide the space, include the latest leadership research, and utilise facilitation processes that enable them to have the conversations they need to have to work together more effectively and take their leadership to the next level.

Cultivated Communities

A number of my programs (virtual or face-to-face), particularly around well-being, have been utilised by local government, state government and other groups as an offering to their community or industry. This partnership approach ensures that my programs are accessible to local communities. They bring people together to cultivate deeper connections and shared learning around key topics of interest.

About the Author

'Leap, and the net will appear' is one of my favourite sayings. John Burroughs' words remind me that the best things I've done in life were initially terrifying, yet they all worked out better than I could have expected. The reward of doing things that stretch and challenge have far outweighed the discomfort.

Cynthia and Alfie

I grew up in Benalla in rural Victoria where my parents owned a vineyard and my Dad worked for the Department of Agriculture. He loved his work and as he was the Unit Manager, we always had interesting people around. This inspired me to pursue a career in agriculture although I could not have imagined I would be where I am now! I have a Master of Agricultural Science, specialising in farm business management economics and rural sociology, and a Bachelor of Agricultural Science.

Even though I started working life as a research economist, I soon discovered a love for facilitation and people development. I've since worked as a facilitator in the dairy, horticulture and mixed farming sectors and as a project manager in biosecurity, the wine industry and in agribusiness. I've also worked with rural women, farm businesses and communities.

After working in state government for seventeen years, I made the leap to start my own leadership practice ten years ago. I've been fortunate to combine my entrepreneurial, creative, colourful and fun spirit with a passion for developing people to be their best and my skills and talent in facilitation, coaching and writing.

I love learning and am constantly researching and studying the latest developments in leadership, team and personal development and incorporating them into my programs. I have a Diploma of Leadership, Coaching and Mentoring, a Certificate IV in Business and Personal Coaching and a Graduate Diploma of Business focused on project and people management. I'm also trained in Dr Brené Brown's Dare To Lead methodology and tools.

My clients range from federal, state and local government to corporates, not-for-profits, small businesses and individuals – all of which share a commitment to growth and development.

Outside of work, the little things make my life very happy. Colour is my delight, and sewing and gardening get my creative juices going. I love to catch up with family and friends, take trips to my hometown of Benalla, and I'm a passionate follower of the Geelong Cats AFL club. Alfie, the cavoodle, means I spend hours at the dog park, chatting to other dog owners. Who knew dog ownership could be such fun!

Let's stay in touch

For more information about my programs, go to www.cynthiamahoney.com.au

I'm on all the socials:

LinkedIn: www.linkedin.com/in/cynthiamahoney/

Twitter: @cynth_mahons

Facebook: www.facebook.com/cynthiamahoneyandassociates

Instagram: @cynthmahoney

If you'd like to subscribe to my fortnightly newsletter, sharing the latest leadership research, stories from the front line and tips and tricks, please visit www.cynthiamahoney.com.au

Finally, if you've read the book and have any thoughts to add, please share them with me.

Email me at cynthia@cynthiamahoney.com.au

References

Achor, S. (2010). ***The Happiness Advantage: the seven principles of positive psychology that fuel success and performance at work.*** New York: Broadway Books.

Achor, S. (2011, June 23). ***The Happiness Dividend.*** Retrieved from Harvard Business Review: https://hbr.org/2011/06/the-happiness-dividend

Achor, S. (2012, March 19). ***Is happiness the secret of success?*** Retrieved 08 21, 2019, from CNN: https://edition.cnn.com/2012/03/19/opinion/happiness-success-achor/index.html

Achor, S. (2012, January). ***Positive Intelligence.*** Retrieved 09 7, 2018, from Harvard Business Review: https://hbr.org/2012/01/positive-intelligence

Achor, S. (2017, January 22). ***We're Better Together.*** Retrieved August 28, 2021, from Live Happy: https://www.livehappy.com/science/were-better-together

Armstrong, J., & Dungate, L. (2011, February). ***The Six Types of Courage***. Retrieved August 24, 2021, from Lion's Whiskers: http://www.lionswhiskers.com/p/six-types-of-courage.html

Australian Bureau of Statistics. (2007). ***National Survey of Mental Health and Wellbeing: Summary of Results 2007***. Retrieved November 3, 2021, from Australian Bureau of Statistics: https://www.abs.gov.au/statistics/health/mental-health/national-survey-mental-health-and-wellbeing-summary-results/latest-release

Australian Human Rights Commission. (2017, March 8). ***A Conversation in Gender Equality (2017).*** Retrieved July

16, 2021, from Australian Human Rights Commission: https://humanrights.gov.au/our-work/sex-discrimination/publications/conversation-gender-equality-2017

Australian Network on Disability. (2018, June 22). ***New National Guidance on Work-related Psychological Health and Safety.*** Retrieved July 30, 2021, from Australian Network on Disability: https://www.and.org.au/news.php/353/new-national-guidance-on-work-related-psychological-health-and-safety,%202018

Barsade, S. (2016, Spring). ***Balancing Emotional and Cognitive Culture***. Retrieved August 30, 2021, from Wharton Magazine: https://magazine.wharton.upenn.edu/issues/spring-2016/balancing-emotional-and-cognitive-culture/

Barsade, S., & O'Neill, O. A. (2016, Jan-Feb). ***Manage Your Emotional Culture.*** Retrieved from Harvard Business Review: https://hbr.org/2016/01/manage-your-emotional-culture

Bianco, M. W., & Nicholson, W. (1975). ***The Velveteen Rabbit: Or, How Toys Become Real.*** New York: Avon Books.

Boaz, N., & Fox, E. A. (2014, March 1). ***Change leader, change thyself***. Retrieved August 29, 2021, from McKinsey Quarterly: https://www.mckinsey.com/featured-insights/leadership/change-leader-change-thyself

Bregman, P. (2018). ***Leading with Emotional Courage: How to have hard conversations, create accountability, and inspire action on your most important work.*** Hoboken: Wiley.

Brown, B. (2010). ***The Gifts of Imperfection: Let Go of Who You Think You're Supposed to Be and Embrace Who You Are***. Center City: Hazelden Publishing.

Brown, B. (2018). ***Dare To Lead.*** London: Vermilion.

Brown, B. (2021). ***Feedback Toolbox Rumble Language***. Retrieved November 3, 2021, from Dare to Lead Hub: https://

brenebrown.com/wp-content/uploads/2021/09/DTL-Cards-Rumble-Language.jpg

Brown, R. M. (1983). ***Sudden Death.*** New York: Bantam Books.

Brown, Z. (2021, May 19). ***@zandashee***. Retrieved October 25, 2021, from Twitter: https://twitter.com/zandashe/status/1394805726825099279?s=20

Caine, C. (2015, March 21). Retrieved October 25, 2021, from Twitter: https://twitter.com/ChristineCaine/status/571814033780682752?s=20

Caldwell, K., & Boyd, C. (2009). Coping and resilience in farming families affected by drought. ***Rural and Remote Health***.

Caprino, K. (2018, December 20). ***How To Build Work Cultures Of Psychological Safety Rather Than Fear***. Retrieved August 1, 2021, from Forbes: https://www.forbes.com/sites/kathycaprino/2018/12/20/how-to-build-work-cultures-of-psychological-safety-rather-than-fear/?sh=bd334b86f69a

Chödrön, P. (2000). ***When Things Fall Apart: Heart Advice for Difficult Times .*** Boston: Shambhala.

Chopra, D. (2018, July 1). ***@DeepakChopra.*** Retrieved from Twitter: https://twitter.com/DeepakChopra/status/1013402730537340929?s=20

Chowdhury, P. (2021, July 7). ***"My Priority Every Single Day": Ashleigh Barty Reveals What's More Important to Her Than Tennis***. Retrieved November 3, 2021, from Essentially Sports: https://www.essentiallysports.com/wta-tennis-news-my-priority-every-single-day-ashleigh-barty-reveals-whats-more-important-to-her-than-tennis/

Clear, J. (2018). ***Atomic Habits: An easy and proven way to build good habits and break bad ones.*** London: Random House UK.

Clear, J. (2021, October 21). ***3-2-1 Thursday newsletter: Trying***

new ideas, preparation, and taking action. Retrieved from James Clear: https://jamesclear.com/3-2-1/october-21-2021

Covey, S. R. (1989). ***The Seven Habits of Highly Effective People.*** New York: Simon & Schuster.

Covey, S. R. (2018, June 10). ***@StephenRCovey***. Retrieved November 3, 2021, from Twitter: https://mobile.twitter.com/stephenrcovey/status/1005449540722483201?lang=en

d.e.b., N. (2010, January 24). ***@debihope***. Retrieved from Twitter: https://twitter.com/debihope/status/8154179378

de Smet, A., Dowling, B., Mugayar-Baldocchi, M., & Schaninger, B. (2021, September 8). ***'Great Attrition' or 'Great Attraction'? The Choice is Yours.*** Retrieved October 22, 2021, from McKinsey & Company: https://www.mckinsey.com/business-functions/people-and-organizational-performance/our-insights/great-attrition-or-great-attraction-the-choice-is-yours

Deloitte. (2019). ***Uncovering talent - a new model for inclusion.*** Retrieved August 29, 2021, from Deloitte: https://www2.deloitte.com/content/dam/Deloitte/us/Documents/about-deloitte/us-about-deloitte-uncovering-talent-a-new-model-of-inclusion.pdf

Deloitte. (2021). ***A Call for Accountability and Action, the Deloitte Global 2021 Millennial and Gen Z Survey.*** Deloitte.

Den Heijer, A. (2018). ***Nothing you don't already know: Remarkable reminders about meaning, purpose, and self-realization.*** Scotts Valley: CreateSpace Independent Publishing Platform. Retrieved from https://www.alexanderdenheijer.com/quotes

Dewar, C., & Doucette, R. (2018, April 9). ***6 elements to create a high-performing culture - What often separates the highest-performing organizations from the rest is culture.*** Retrieved June 28, 2021, from McKinsey & Company: https://www.

mckinsey.com/business-functions/organization/our-insights/the-organization-blog/6-elements-to-create-a-high-performing-culture

Dollard, M., Bailey, T., McLinton, S., Richards, P., McTernan, W., Taylor, A., & Bond, S. (2012, December). ***The Australian Workplace Barometer: Report on psychosocial safety climate and worker health in Australia.*** Retrieved August 2021, from Safe Work Australia: https://www.safeworkaustralia.gov.au/system/files/documents/1702/the-australian-workplace-barometer-report.pdf

Dominee. (2021, July 10). ***@blessingmanifesting***. Retrieved July 10, 2021, from Instagram: https://www.instagram.com/p/CRJT5WfjEXN/?utm_medium=copy_link

Doshi, D. (2017). Traits and Characteristics of Leaders in a Rural and Remote Health Service Area in Australia. ***Joint Event on 2nd International Conference on Healthcare & Hospital Management and 6th International Conference on Medical & Nursing Education.*** Vienna: Health Care : Current Reviews. Retrieved July 15, 2020, from Longdom Publishing SL: https://www.longdom.org/proceedings/traits-and-characteristics-of-leaders-in-a-rural-and-remote-health-service-area-in-australia-10915.html

Dowd, M. (2018, September 8). ***Lady of the Rings: Jacinda Rules***. Retrieved August 7, 2021, from New York Times: https://www.nytimes.com/2018/09/08/opinion/sunday/jacinda-ardern-new-zealand-prime-minister.html

Doyle, G. (2020). ***Untamed, Stop Pleasing, Start Living.*** London: Penguin Random House UK.

Drew, D. C. (2021, June 25). ***The 6 Types Of Courage – With Examples***. Retrieved August 24, 2021, from HelpfulProfessor.com: https://helpfulprofessor.com/types-of-courage/

DS Psychology. (2017). ***Four Steps for Assertive Communication***. Retrieved November 3, 2021, from DS Psychology: https://dspsychology.com.au/four-steps-for-assertive-communication/

Dweck, C. (2007). ***Mindset: The New Psychology of Success.*** New York: Ballantine Books.

Edmondson, A. C. (2019). ***The Fearless Organization: creating psychological safety in the workplace for learning, innovation and growth.*** Hoboken, NJ: Wiley.

Elkanne, A. (2018, April 1). ***Minouche Shafik***. Retrieved August 28, 2021, from Alaine Elkann Interviews: https://www.alainelkanninterviews.com/minouche-shafik/

Eurich, T. (2017). ***Insight: How to suceed by seeing yourself clearly.*** London: Pan Books.

Fernandez, C. (2019, January 8). ***12 Audre Lorde Quotes That'll Spark Conversation***. Retrieved August 6, 2021, from Oprah Daily: https://www.oprahdaily.com/life/relationships-love/g25776736/audre-lorde-quotes/?slide=4

Fire Up Coaching. (2015). Neuroleadership. ***Diploma of Leadership, Coaching and Mentoring - Learning Module 5, Version 7***. Melbourne, Victoria, Australia: Fire Up Coaching.

Flade, P., Asplund, J., & Elliot, G. (2015, October 8). ***Employees Who Use Their Strengths Outperform Those Who Don't***. Retrieved August 28, 2021, from Gallup Workplace: https://www.gallup.com/workplace/236561/employees-strengths-outperform-don.aspx

Fredrickson, B. (n.d.). ***History of Happiness***. Retrieved 04 6, 2019, from Pursuit of Happiness: https://www.pursuit-of-happiness.org/history-of-happiness/barb-fredrickson/

Fredrickson, B. L. (2009). ***Positivity: Top notch research reveals the 3-to-1 ratio that will change your life.*** New York: Harmony.

Gallup. (2021, October). ***State of the Global Workplace: 2021 Report.*** Retrieved from Gallup : https://www.gallup.com/workplace/349484/state-of-the-global-workplace.aspx

Gaston, M. (2017). ***The Art of Wellbeing: Joyous living inspired by nature.*** Melbourne: Hardie Grant Books.

Gaston, M. (2020). ***At Home Within: A Little Book of Self-Care Wisdom.*** Melbourne: Hardie Grant Books.

Glaser, J. E. (2014). ***Conversational Intelligence: how great leaders build trust and get extraordinary results.*** New York: Bibliomotion Inc.

Glaser, J. E. (2016, June 14). ***Go the Distance! From Distrust to Trust.*** Retrieved 07 15, 2021, from Psychology Today: https://www.psychologytoday.com/au/blog/conversational-intelligence/201606/go-the-distance-distrust-trust

Goldsmith, M. (2008). ***What Got You Here Won't Get You There.*** London: Profile Books.

Goldsmith, M. (2017, August). ***6 Things You Don't Ever Want Your Co-Workers to Hear You Say***. Retrieved November 3, 2021, from Marshall Goldsmith: https://marshallgoldsmith.com/articles/6-things-you-dont-ever-want-your-co-workers-to-hear-you-say/

Goleman, D. (2000, March-April). ***Leadership That Gets Results.*** Retrieved 2020, from Harvard Business Review: https://hbr.org/2000/03/leadership-that-gets-results

Google. (2021). ***Guide: Understand team effectiveness.*** Retrieved August 30, 2020, from re:work: https://rework.withgoogle.com/print/guides/5721312655835136/

Gordon, A. (1935). Interview with an Immortal. ***Readers Digest***.

Grenny, J. (2014, May 30). ***The Best Teams Hold Themselves Accountable***. Retrieved August 29, 2021, from Harvard Business Review: https://hbr.org/2014/05/the-best-teams-hold-themselves-accountable

Hall, J. W. (2004). ***Conversations with Audre Lorde.*** Jackson: University Press of Mississippi.

Henderson, M. (2014). ***Above the Line.*** Richond: John Wiley & Sons Australia.

Hernández, J. G. (2020, May 17). ***Leadership Summaries.*** Retrieved 7 24, 2021, from The Yerkes-Dodson Law: https://jesusgilhernandez.com/2020/05/17/yerkes-dodson-law/

Hill, D. (2021, August). ***Darren Hill***. Retrieved November 3, 2021, from LinkedIn: https://www.linkedin.com/posts/fromdarrenhill_workplaceculture-teamculture-activity-6820836218905890816-jO4s

Kellogg, R. (2020, November 2). ***The Authenticity Myth: What Authentic Cultures Are Really Made Of***. Retrieved August 29, 2021, from Forbes: https://www.forbes.com/sites/forbeshumanresourcescouncil/2020/11/02/the-authenticity-myth-what-authentic-cultures-are-really-made-of/?sh=37e52e187a00

Kelly, F. (2021, May 18). ***Australia finally adopts a work and family policy blueprint***. Retrieved May 18, 2021, from ABC Radio National: https://www.abc.net.au/radionational/programs/breakfast/australia-finally-adopts-a-work-and-family-policy-blueprint/13348514

Lerner, H. G. (1985). ***The Dance of Anger: A Woman's Guide to Changing the Patterns of Intimate Relationships.*** New York: Harper & Row.

Lewis, C. (2021, August 3). ***Blokes, barbecue, bonfire, beers, bonding and bullshit: The six B's helping to improve men's health in the bush***. Retrieved August 6, 2021, from ABC News: https://www.abc.net.au/news/2021-08-03/6b-farmers-checking-in-with-each-other-western-australia/100343310

Lindburg, C. (2021). ***Pacesetting Leadership – What is it?***

Pros/Cons? Examples? Retrieved March 15, 2021, from Leadership Ahoy!: https://www.leadershipahoy.com/pacesetting-leadership-what-is-it-pros-cons-examples/

Maclaren, I. (1897). ***Quotes of famous people***. Retrieved October 24, 2021, from Quote Park: https://quotepark.com/quotes/836979-ian-maclaren-be-kind-for-everyone-you-meet-is-fighting-a-hard/

Martin, S. (2021, August 29). ***Soul Unique***. Retrieved November 3, 2021, from Facebook: https://www.facebook.com/hashtag/staciemartin

McEwan, B. S., & Mirsky, A. E. (2018, March). ***Toxic Stress and Brain Development: Understanding Resilience.*** Retrieved October 29, 2021, from Mt Sinai Adolescent Health Centre: https://www.teenhealthcare.org/wp-content/uploads/2018/03/McEwen-_MSSM_Adolescent_Brain_2018fn-v2.pdf

McQuaid, M. (2021). ***The Positive Psychology Practitioner's Toolkit***. Retrieved August 30, 2021, from The Well-Being Lab: https://www.michellemcquaid.com/positive-psychology-practitioners-toolkit/

Microsoft. (2021). ***The Work Trend Index.*** Retrieved from Microsoft: https://www.microsoft.com/en-us/worklab/work-trend-index

Mohr, T. (2020). ***10 Rules For Brilliant Women.*** Retrieved from Tara Mohr: https://www.taramohr.com/10-rules/

National Rural Health Alliance Inc. (2017, December). ***Mental Health in Rural and Remote Australia Fact Sheet December 2017.*** Retrieved July 17, 2021, from National Rural Health Alliance: https://www.ruralhealth.org.au/sites/default/files/publications/nrha-mental-health-factsheet-dec-2017.pdf

Neff, K. (2015, September 30). ***The Five Myths of Self-Compassion.*** Retrieved August 30, 2021, from Greater Good

Magazine: https://greatergood.berkeley.edu/article/item/the_five_myths_of_self_compassion

Netflix. (2021). ***Netflix Culture***. Retrieved August 30, 2021, from Netflix Jobs: https://jobs.netflix.com/culture

Newport Academy. (2018, June 8). ***The Mental Health Benefits of Compassion***. Retrieved August 8, 2021, from Newport Academy: https://www.newportacademy.com/resources/well-being/compassion-benefits/

Nisen, M. (2013, June 18). ***Hubspot CEO: 99% Of Corporate Cultures Are Stuck In The Past.*** Retrieved from Business Insider: https://www.businessinsider.com.au/hubspot-ceo-brian-halligan-on-company-culture-2013-6?r=US&IR=T

Orr, J. E. (2012). ***Proof Point: Survival of the most self-aware.*** Retrieved 10 20, 2021, from The Korn/Ferry Institute: https://www.kornferry.com/content/dam/kornferry/docs/article-migration/Survival%20of%20the%20most%20self-aware-%20Nearly%2080%20percent%20of%20leaders%20have%20blind%20spots%20about%20their%20skills%20.pdf

Penhart, S. (2020, August 21). ***Developing and Sustaining High-Performance Work Teams***. Retrieved October 22, 2021, from Penhard Performance Group: https://penhartperformance.com/shrm-developing-and-sustaining-high-performance-work-teams/

Peters, T. (2021). ***Excellence Now: extreme humanism.*** Chicago: Networlding Publishing.

Philanthropy Australia. (2021). ***What leadership looks like beyond the nations cities and suburbs***. Retrieved November 3, 2021, from Philanthropy Australia: https://www.philanthropy.org.au/stories-rural-leadership/

Popova, M. (2015, March 30). ***Enormous Smallness: The Sweet Illustrated Story of E. E. Cummings and His Creative Bravery***.

Retrieved November 3, 2021, from The Marginalian: https://www.themarginalian.org/2015/03/30/enormous-smallness-e-e-cummings-matthew-burgess/

Porath, C. (2019). ***Why being respectful to your coworkers is good for business***. Retrieved August 30, 2021, from TEDx University of Nevada: https://www.ted.com/talks/christine_porath_why_being_respectful_to_your_coworkers_is_good_for_business?language=en

Porath, C., & Pearson, C. (2013). ***The Price of Incivility***. Retrieved August 28, 2021, from Harvard Business Review: https://hbr.org/2013/01/the-price-of-incivility

R U OK? (2021). ***R U OK?*** Retrieved October 22, 2021, from R U OK?: https://www.ruok.org.au/what-were-about

Razzetti, G. (2019, June 28). ***Practical ways to start building trust and collaboration***. Retrieved August 29, 2021, from Fearless Culture: https://www.fearlessculture.design/blog-posts/how-to-build-a-culture-of-psychological-safety

Safe Work Australia. (2019, January). ***Work-related Psychological Health and Safety: a systematic aproach to meeting your duties.*** Retrieved June 6, 2021, from Safe Work Australia: https://www.safeworkaustralia.gov.au/system/files/documents/1911/work-related_psychological_health_and_safety_a_systematic_approach_to_meeting_your_duties.pdf

Seeger, P. (1965). Turn! Turn! Turn! [Recorded by T. Byrds].

Seuss, D. (1990). ***Oh, the Places You'll Go!*** New York: Penguin Random House LLC.

Stephens, A. (2018, December 20). ***5 Causes of Psychological Injury in the Workplace and How to Avoid Them***. Retrieved July 2021, 15, from People Sense: https://www.peoplesense.com.au/news/article/20122018-453/5-causes-of-psychological-injury-in-the-workplace-and-how-to-avoid-them

Swift, T., Martin, M., & Shellback (1989). ***Shake It Off*** [Recorded by T. Swift].

Taylor, C. (2021). ***Building Confidence in Your Culture.*** Retrieved September 20, 2021, from Walking the Talk: https://www.walkingthetalk.com/building-confidence-in-your-culture-report

The Conscious Leadership Group. (2014, November 16). ***Locating Yourself - A Key to Conscious Leadership***. Retrieved June 21, 2016, from You Tube: https://www.youtube.com/watch?v=fLqzYDZAqCI

The Creating WE Institute. (2021). ***C-IQ Neuro-Tip Cards & Facilitator Guide***. Retrieved November 3, 2021, from The Creating WE Institute: https://creatingwe.com/products/c-iq-neuro-tip-cards-facilitator-guide

The Well-Being Lab. (2021). ***The State of Well-Being in Michigan Communities.*** The Well-Being Lab.

Thesaurus, R. 2. (2013). Retrieved February 8, 2021, from Roget's 21st Century Thesaurus Third Edition Copyright : https://www.thesaurus.com/browse/high%20performance

Thompson, S. (2020, April 22). Well-Being Wednesday. (C. Mahoney, Interviewer)

Thorbecke, C. (2021, July 2). ***Why business leaders need a 'wake-up call' to take burnout seriously right now, experts say***. Retrieved August 28, 2021, from ABC News: https://abcnews.go.com/Business/business-leaders-wake-call-burnout-now-experts/story?id=78447873

Total SDI. (2018). Total SDI. ***Strength Deployment Inventory Facilitator's Notes***.

Trzeciak, S., & Mazzarelli, A. (2019). ***Compassionomics: The Revolutionary Scientific Evidence that Caring Makes a Difference.*** Pensacola: Studer Group.

VIA Institute on Character. (2021). ***Bring Your Strengths to Life & Live More Fully***. Retrieved August 30, 2021, from VIA Institute on Character: https://www.viacharacter.org/

Wambach, A. (2019). ***Wolfpack: How to Come Together, Unleash Our Power, and Change the Game.*** London: Piatkus.

Weir, K. (2012). The Pain of Social Rejection. ***American Psychological Association***, 50.

Wheatley, M. J. (2005). ***How is Your Leadership Changing?*** Retrieved August 8, 2021, from Margaret J. Wheatley/ Writings: https://www.margaretwheatley.com/articles/howisyourleadership.html

Wilkinson, D. (2017). ***The difference between organisational culture and climate and why it matters.*** Retrieved August 30, 2021, from The Oxford Review Briefings: https://oxford-review.com/blog-research-difference-culture-climate/

Williamson, M. (1996). ***A Return to Love.*** New York: HarperCollins.

Wolfson, R. (2017, October 31). ***Uncovering The Two Keys To Leadership Legacy.*** Retrieved from Huff Post: https://www.huffpost.com/entry/uncovering-the-two-keys-to-leadership-legacy_b_59f89e89e4b0de896d3f2b7e

Worksafe. (2017, June). ***Tractor rollover protection structures (ROPS) - Requirements.*** Retrieved August 1, 2021, from Worksafe: https://www.worksafe.vic.gov.au/resources/tractor-rollover-protection-structures-rops-requirements

World Health Organization. (2019, May 28). ***Burn-out an "occupational phenomenon": International Classification of Diseases.*** Retrieved March 15, 2021, from World Health Organization: https://www.who.int/news/item/28-05-2019-burn-out-an-occupational-phenomenon-international-classification-of-diseases

APPENDIX 1

Behaviours for Rural Leaders to Eliminate

Top-down leadership

Dominating

Patriarchal

Authoritarian – 'my way or the highway'

Nepotism, overlooking talent in favour of who they know

Micromanagement

Like selecting like (no diversity)

Exclude others

Combative

Talk the talk but rarely walk the walk

Undermine others

See others as threats

Opposed to listening

Stomp on people to get ahead

Financial concerns dominate decision-making

Boys' club mentality – it's strong and should be gone

Fearful of community engagement

Limited creativity – 'This is how it's always been done.' Not adapting or willing to adopt new ideas or technology

Arrogance

Shy away from difficult conversations and decisions

Bullies rise to the top – just like ***The Hunger Games***

Lack of integrity

Push people to their absolute limits to see how much they can get out of them

Unaccountable for mistakes

Unwilling to change course as new information comes to light

Dehumanise staff

Not living by values and values as tokenism

Self-importance

Unwilling to support employees in maintaining a healthy work-life balance

Self-interest above all else – feathering their own nest

Professional badge-wearers – on every committee, but never put in the hours or get their boots dirty. Our committee or community is just a rung on their ladder to the next badge

Unresponsive to others

The traditional masculine model of leadership

Have to know everything, always need to be right

Make ad hoc decisions

Lack integrity

Deliberate and unconscious poor behaviour to women in the workplace

Evade accountability

Blame and shame others

Bombastic, big-noting

Tokenism

Make people fearful

Listen to gossip, talk about the staff behind their backs and undermine people

Promote a culture of secrecy

A façade of collaboration that is just platitudes

Big egos and domineering – too often, it's all about personal interests

Put people down

Punish people for calling out poor behaviour

Undermine others' confidence

Sexist – men in our town still challenge and try to chop down women who dare to step up

APPENDIX 2

Behaviours for Rural Leaders to Cultivate

Challenge us to be our best

Be open to suggestions and change

Coach

Listen to people from all walks of life – try to understand all sides of each story

Mentor and help others grow and develop

An inclusive and process-driven collaborative approach

Honest

Humble

Willing to share

Servant leadership

Put collective outcomes above self-interest

Approachable

Calm

Allow staff to have a go and make mistakes but step in to help when necessary.

Never become defensive or irritated when provided with feedback or recommendations to improve

Build people up

Tell the truth no matter how difficult

Be there in good times and bad

Generous

Authentic

Talk the talk. Walk the walk

Relatable and caring

Advocate for others

Integrity, honourable and principled

Fair

True representation

Bring people together to make positive change that is inclusive of the community

Get the job done

Mentor empathetically and genuinely want others to do well. Open doors and offer a hand up in career and profession

Kind

Lead from within and not above, and bring others along with them

Be clear about expectations

Step up and be brave

Considerate of others

Provide support and encouragement for all staff to grow and move forwards

Accountable

Collaborate

Play the game, not the person

Innovative

Imperfect

More ownership of our own experience, and permission to be a leader to ourselves and others

Select women and different cultures with equal skills and abilities or even more

Sense of humour

See a problem and set about finding solutions

Always have an open-door policy

Make decisions in a timely fashion

Communicate openly but constructively

Admit limited knowledge of an issue

Think about the needs of the larger community, not your own

Focus on building other people up, not tearing them down to make the leader look good

Inclusive, act as a community instead of having lots of little groups that don't talk to each other

Focus on delivering on what our industry needs rather than politicking and back-scratching

Trust the team and don't micromanage

www.ingramcontent.com/pod-product-compliance
Lightning Source LLC
Chambersburg PA
CBHW040753220326
41597CB00029BA/4749

9780645355109